£1·25

The Book of Rock-Climbing

In recent years rock-climbing has not only become one of Britain's most popular outdoor sports, it has also made tremendous advances in technique and equipment. Climbs which were considered impossible twenty years ago are now climbed regularly each weekend by young experts.

This book, specially written for the boy or girl novice, retains all that is best in traditional rock-climbing but adds to it the newer skills of the last decade, with the result that it becomes a thorough, up to the minute, guide to the sport.

The author has spent many years teaching rock-climbing to beginners of all ages, so that he can pin-point with accuracy the techniques and situations where help is most needed. He discusses frankly the costs involved, choice of companions and the exciting moment of a first lead, when a novice takes his first command of a rope.

The equipment of the sport is given comprehensive coverage with emphasis on newly tested materials and safety factors. Safety and enjoyment are keynotes throughout.

Above all this is an intensely practical book where abstract ideas are backed up by numerous examples from British crags.

Walt Unsworth

The Book of
Rock-Climbing

ARTHUR BARKER LIMITED
5 Winsley Street London W1

SBN 213 17642 4

Phototypeset by BAS Printers Limited, Wallop, Hampshire
and printed by Unwin Brothers Limited, Woking

Contents

Illustrations

Preface

The purpose of this book is to provide young people with an introduction to the safe enjoyment of rock-climbing. It is also intended to help those, who though good climbers themselves, are faced with the task of instructing others for the first time.

Fundamentally, the book deals with the two aspects of modern climbing – skills and protection, and develops each from its simplest beginnings. Blind acceptance of 'rules' is not enough in this sport: understanding is vital.

Examples are quoted from a wide variety of crags throughout Britain: climbs of proven quality and interest for novices under instruction. A certain emphasis is also placed on outcrop climbing, for outcrops are easily accessible and of great value in learning skills.

The line drawings and the photographs of figures 5, 10, 14, 22 and 25 are my own. For figures 1, 2, 12c, 15, 29 and 30, I am indebted to Ellis Brigham Ltd of Manchester. The bulk of the illustrations, however, are the work of Mr R. H. Heaton, to whom my thanks are specially due.

W. Unsworth,
Worsley, Manchester.

1　The World of Climbing

Hundreds of feet above me, on what appeared to be rocks as steep as the walls of a house, they moved slowly backwards and forwards, but always getting higher, till they finally reached the summit. I knew nothing about climbing and it seemed to me perfectly marvellous that human beings should be able to do such things.

Norman Collie, who wrote those words many years ago, went on to become one of the best rock-climbers of his day. He expresses the wonder and excitement which most young people feel when they see climbers in action, and like Collie, many are so enthralled that they take up the sport themselves and find that they are absorbed in a new world – the world of climbing.

In fact, climbing is more than a sport; it is a way of life. There is something about steep crags which offers a perpetual challenge, and though you may know that a climb has been done a hundred or a thousand times before, until you tackle it personally it is still a challenge. Then too there are the rocks which have never been climbed – this is where the expert finds his challenge, especially if some other expert has pronounced the climb 'impossible'! There are long climbs and short climbs, easy ones and hard ones, climbs to tax the strength of young supermen and climbs which are gentle, yet so beautiful that elderly gentlemen repeat them year after year.

Climbing is so absorbing that keen climbers rush off to the hills immediately school or work is finished on Friday night and do not come back until late on Sunday, every weekend of the year. Most of them are hard up and live frugally so that they can afford their precious time in the hills. They stay in club huts, or camp, or in summer even bivouac, hoping that the weather will be kind, but not caring much if it isn't. If they can afford it, the summer holiday is spent on some major adventure – the Alps perhaps – but their staple diet is long June evenings climbing on the local outcrops and weekends in Wales or the Lake District.

They are a friendly bunch, often argumentative and given to telling tall stories (like fishermen!) and they come from every walk of life. The chap you see leading Central Buttress may be a bricklayer, or he may be a professor of astrophysics – there is no way of distinguishing them in their scruffy climbing gear. Above all, they are friendly to beginners, especially to beginners who show a willingness to learn the sport properly. With fools who act dangerously they can be very hard indeed!

Not so many years ago the climbing world was a small one which was difficult to enter. A youngster who wanted to start climbing had to fend very much for himself; either he went climbing alone, or he persuaded a friend to go with him, using his mother's 'borrowed' clothes-line for a rope. Many of our most famous climbers started in this way but, as you can well imagine, it was very dangerous and many would-be climbers must have given up in despair.

Solo climbing, as climbing alone is called, is often indulged in by competent cragsmen when they wish to keep in trim and they have no companions, but such climbers know full well the extra risks they are running and they usually take care to climb within their limits. For a novice it is far too dangerous: the confident quickly become over-confident and the nervous have what little confidence they started with drained away. Only a complete fool will tell you that there are no dangers in climbing: the whole point of the game is to overcome difficulty whilst reducing danger to an acceptable level.

There is now no need for anybody to start climbing without assistance. In the last few years clubs have mushroomed, even in the most unlikely places, and many of them are willing to accept young novices and train them. In addition, many schools and youth clubs have climbing groups and quite a number of local education authorities maintain their own mountain centres, where rock-climbing and allied activities are taught.

Nearly all climbing clubs hold beginners' meets, during which a whole weekend is given over specifically to training novices, but local clubs are essentially friendly bodies and even on their ordinary meets it is quite usual for novices to be asked to join a rope on easier climbs.

Of course, the quality of instruction varies enormously. It is seldom systematic and never formal, but if you approach it in a critical frame of mind, you can learn quite a lot in a short time.

Unfortunately, there are some climbers who will take absolute novices on the most hair-raising of ascents because they foolishly believe in 'dropping 'em in the deep end'. I remember once there was a young man who was madly keen to go climbing, so at last an experienced climber took him to Borrowdale and led him up Troutdale Pinnacle Direct; a Very Severe and exposed climb. The effect was so frightening on the beginner that all his enthusiasm vanished and he never climbed again. Keep off the harder climbs until you are quite sure you can climb them properly.

Another popular way to begin climbing is to join one of the many introductory courses that are now available. The advantage here is that the instruction is systematic and concentrated, and the instructor will have considerable experience in teaching people how to climb. Usually the courses last for a week or a fortnight at one of the famous climbing centres, and these can be fairly expensive, depending largely on the accommodation provided. The CCPR however, also run local courses, and so do some education authorities, where the instruction is spread over several weekends and takes place on local outcrops. These are considerably cheaper.

In Britain the advisory body for all aspects of climbing is the British Mountaineering Council (usually known as the BMC). It is comprised of representatives of member clubs and its duties are wide ranging, from the testing of new equipment to negotiating access to private land. It will also advise beginners on clubs and training facilities. You will find its address at the end of this book.

What does a training course, or a club, expect of its members in the way of physical fitness? One of the common myths about climbers is that they are all big burly types who love to go charging about the hills with rucksacks weighing half a ton. Nothing could be further from the truth. Some of our best rock-climbers are quite small men in stature, and there are a lot of girl climbers who would resent it very much if you called them big and burly! The real truth is that height and weight are of little consequence; what matters most is power to weight ratio – and that only on the harder climbs.

A general level of fitness is necessary for rock-climbing just as it is for any outdoor activity, but superb physical fitness such as you see in gymnasts is certainly not required – which is just as well, or ninety-nine per cent of climbers would be looking for a new sport tomorrow! In the early stages a reasonable agility and a sense of balance are the prime requirements, though on some of the longer and harder climbs, finger strength and stamina are useful.

There are very few climbers who actually do gym exercises to keep fit, because most exercises bear very little relation to the sport and since climbing is a year round activity there is no such thing as 'out of season training'.

What have emerged in the last few years, however, are various types of 'climbing walls', specifically designed to improve actual climbing skills. These are of two types – the portable or semi-portable frame covered in thick plywood with holds which are screwed on, and the more elaborate wall which is specially built into the end of an existing gym. Many schools and colleges are now being equipped with sports-halls, one wall of which is usually devoted to rock-climbing.

A climbing wall can be an invaluable asset in learning the basic skills and procedures: for example, belaying and rope management can be learnt without using up the valuable time available at the actual rocks, but they are not a true substitute for the real thing.

A climbing wall can also be of material assistance in helping someone to overcome a fear of heights. Vertigo is a strange affliction, very real for some people and extremely frightening. I am sure that it can be overcome by gradual acclimatisation to height and sheerness – what climbers call exposure, but the emphasis must be on the word gradual. I was once asked by a young man whether I could cure him of vertigo, and it was such an unusual challenge that I took on the job. I used a climbing wall and some small gritstone crags. Whether I was completely successful I have no way of knowing, but before he left me he was climbing thirty-foot slabs without a tremor of fear.

Perhaps vertigo is one of the many facets of confidence which enter into climbing. Certain it is that confidence makes climbing more enjoyable, and this is one of the reasons why I believe that any rock-climbing beginner should start in summer, when the rocks are warm and bathed in sunshine. Technique apart, a beginner should revel in the sheer joy of climbing steep rocks – and he is unlikely to do that if his fingers are frozen.

As a member of a club you will be expected to provide your own climbing equipment and on most courses you are expected to provide at least the personal items. Most climbers acquire the basic equipment as soon as possible and then collect the rest bit by bit as their needs and experience grows. This is certainly the best way – even if you have the necessary money, it is not a good idea to rush out and buy everything you can think of; quite often you will choose the wrong thing – like a keen chap I once knew who turned up at the foot of the Milestone Buttress in Wales one bright summer's day carrying an ice-axe and crampons.

Of course, if you have an experienced friend who is willing to take you out for a day on some local outcrop you need no more than some old sports clothes, an anorak, and a pair of plimsolls, since he would provide the technical gear such as rope. However, most people are not so fortunate and must fend for themselves, so here is a list of the gear you are likely to need the first few times you go climbing:

Boots
Windproof clothing
Climbing helmet
Rucksack
Rope

Two or three slings and karabiners
Waistlength
Guide book(s), map(s) and compass
Small first-aid kit, including torch and whistle

We can talk about most of this gear, and more specialised equipment, when we come to discuss its use in climbing, but the first four items in the list are so vital and personal that I intend to deal with them straight away. They should be your first acquisitions.

A glance through a recent catalogue shows me that the firm in question is offering no less than twenty-eight different styles of climbing boot! True, some of them are high altitude boots costing a small fortune, but even so the remainder leaves a bewildering choice for the novice.

The boots which you choose will have to fulfill two main purposes. The first is that they must get you to and from the crags in comfort under any kind of weather conditions, and the second is that they must provide a secure grip on steep rocks. For a young beginner, whose feet may still be growing, it is a waste of money to buy the more expensive and specialised climbing boots with all their refinements: a compromise is the walking-cum-climbing boot put out for general mountain wear, and costing several pounds less; they are quite adequate for all but the hardest climbs. Such a boot, for example, is the popular 'Helvellyn' by Hawkins, which costs between £6 and £7.

Boots nowadays are very much more comfortable than they were a few years ago, but it is still important to make sure that they are a good fit. With the cheaper boots it is probably better to wear two pairs of woollen socks (many British climbers do this anyway) and so you should be wearing two pairs when you try on the boots in the shop. Boots should be snug but not tight; sufficient room just to wriggle your toes.

Other points to look for are their waterproof qualities and a good moulded rubber sole such as Vibram or Commando. Nailed boots are seldom used these days, for though they have certain admirable qualities, the advantages of the rubber sole outweigh them. If the boots are purchased

from one of the recognised dealers in climbing equipment, these points will be taken care of and you will get expert advice on the fit. Industrial boots, baseball boots and shoes are not satisfactory for climbing.

Amongst the expert rock-climbers, boots like those I have just described are rather disparagingly known as 'bendy boots' because they do not have the stiffened sole like the pure rock-climbing boot. The stiffening is done by inserting a metal or plastic shank along the boot and it has the effect of making the soles more positive on small holds. Boots such as these are much more expensive than general mountain boots but the difference is such that a beginner is not likely to benefit much. Rock-climbing boots can come later, when you are expert enough to appreciate their advantages. By that time your original boots will be fairly worn out anyway, and they can be relegated to 'trog boots', for general knocking around in the valleys. The features of a good rock-climbing boot are shown in figure 1.

Modern boots are very comfortable and do not usually need breaking-in, but if you are not accustomed to wearing boots it is a good idea to get used to them gradually. Try wearing them for an hour each day and going for short walks in them until they feel perfectly comfortable.

It is important, too, that boots are well cared for. They should never be put away dirty or wet. They should be wiped dry with a cloth, newspaper stuffed inside them and placed in a draught. A fire is fatal – my very first boots were placed in front of a roaring fire to dry them and the result was that they were baked as hard as the rocks they were meant to climb! Once your boots are dried they should be brushed with a stiff brush, stones prised from the moulded sole, and then given a good coating of wax polish. From time to time the laces should be checked for wear, and a spare pair of laces is a useful addition to carry on a day's outing.

An experienced climber always hopes for good weather but prepares for the worst. Our weather in Britain is so fickle, especially in mountainous areas, that it seldom remains settled for long and when it turns bad it can be very bad indeed, and a climber needs adequate protection against it.

The main aim is to keep your body at a reasonable temperature so that in hot weather you do not suffer from heat exhaustion, and in cold conditions you do not suffer from exposure. This is achieved by loose fitting windproof clothing. Loose fitting, because in summer it allows the air to circulate around your body, removing perspiration and keeping you cool, whilst in winter, trapped beneath an anorak, these same layers of air provide effective insulation. Windproof, rather than rainproof, because it is the piercing winds which reduce body temperature. Getting wet, on the other hand, is not nearly so bad, providing you can keep warm.

This is one reason why wool is the best material for mountain clothing; when it is wet it still retains its warmth whereas cotton or nylon does not. Hence the most suitable clothes for a day in the hills would be woollen underclothes (boys may prefer a string vest which is even warmer), a woollen shirt, woollen sweater, flannel or wool trousers, and long woollen stockings.

Such clothing would be fairly typical for an average summer's day, though quite obviously, if it was a very warm day the sweater would be kept in your rucksack. In fact many climbers prefer to carry two sweaters; a light one and a heavier one of Norwegian oiled wool.

Shorts offer no protection at all from exposure and are useful only for walking along hot valleys. The same thing applies to girls' skirts, of course, and when it comes to actual rock-climbing, shorts and skirts offer no protection from the abrasiveness of the rock. Neither are denim jeans much use to a climber. They are not windproof and they do not retain body heat when they are wet. For a day at the local outcrop this would not matter very much, but another disadvantage of jeans is that they are much too tight fitting to allow the sort of movement a climber needs.

An old pair of flannels, or wool/terylene slacks are the best for your early climbing days, though it will not be long before you see the advantages of properly designed climbing breeches. These are made for both men and women and they allow one's legs to be freely moved without that cluttered feeling produced by trouser legs. The best materials for climbing breeches are Bedford cord or Moleskin, and points to look out for are that they should be a comfortable fit (never buy without first trying them on), have a double textured seat, deep and covered pockets, and easy fastenings below the knees. Breeches incorporating all these features can be bought for about £4 (see figure 2).

Final protection from bad weather is given by an anorak or smock; perhaps the most important single item of equipment after boots.

Anoraks are so common these days that there is no need for me to go into a description of this useful garment, but it might be worth bearing in mind that they are not all of good quality. Some are virtually anoraks in name only – play jacket would be a better name – and the best that can be said for them as regards climbing is that they are better than nothing. Remember, an anorak should be windproof (none of them are waterproof) and this is only achieved by using material such as Ventile cloth or special poplin. Features to look for in a good anorak, cloth apart, are

Figure 2
CLIMBING BREECHES. This young lady is
properly kitted out for climbing yet still
looks smart. Notice the lightweight
kletterschuhe.

double or triple textured shoulders, an easy but windproof
neck fastening, a generous hood (for going over a helmet),
and elasticated inner cuffs ('stormproof').

Unfortunately most anoraks are still manufactured in
dark colours, which can be a disadvantage if the wearer
ever has to be rescued – it is so much easier to spot bright
colours on a drab mountainside. I am sure that this will
soon change, and in fact, anoraks at the moment are the
subject of much experimenting, with new 'improved' models
appearing almost each month.

But I must confess that I have not owned an anorak at
all for the last five years or so. Like many climbers I have
switched my allegiance to the lightweight polyurethane
smock known by its French name of cagoule. At first
these smocks were intended simply as a waterproof cover
to go over an anorak, but they very quickly came to replace
the anorak itself as the polyurethane material was improved
and made more wearing. At the moment of writing a heavier

20

grade of material is coming on to the market which should make them more hard-wearing still.

Cagoules are so light that they will roll up and fit in a trouser pocket, but despite their flimsy appearance they are windproof and waterproof. Their disadvantages, at the moment, are that they do not last as long as a good anorak because the proofing seems to wear off, and, since they are waterproof, they can cause body moisture to condense *inside* the garment. But they are brightly coloured and fairly cheap, and their good qualities outweigh their bad.

Choose a cagoule that is loose-fitting and fairly long in the skirt. You should be able to sit on the hem and pull the front of the skirt over your knees. The value of this will not be fully appreciated until you have to sit on a ledge in heavy rain, or perhaps undergo an involuntary bivouac.

Waterproof overtrousers have never found much favour with rock-climbers because they cause a terrible amount of condensation – much more than a cagoule, in my experience. Nevertheless they are worth taking along as extra protection whenever you are visiting some particularly remote cliff and especially in winter. They can easily be carried in a rucksack and regarded as 'emergency gear'.

Here are some typical weights and prices of overgarments:

Polyurethane cagoule	9 oz	£4
Poplin anorak	32 oz	£6
Ventile anorak	32 oz	£12
Overtrousers	8 oz	£2

Until quite recently the suggestion that climbers should wear protective helmets was not taken very seriously and you will still see many climbers without one. Statistics show, however, that head injuries are the most common factor in serious climbing accidents and so it is only good sense to wear a helmet.

Remember, a helmet has two advantages: it can prevent injury in case of a fall, and equally important, it can prevent an accident altogether by protecting your head against falling stones. Even a small stone, falling from a height, has sufficient force to temporarily stun a climber if he is not wearing a helmet.

Figure 3
A Climbing Helmet

At the time of writing there are no standards laid down for helmets, but they should be of fibre-glass, close-fitting (preferably without brim) and have a sound and comfortable fastening. The point about the fastening is that it should not allow the helmet to come off in the event of a fall. Industrial helmets, such as those worn at building sites, have inadequate fastenings, but they are certainly better than nothing and cost only a few shillings. Proper climbing helmets cost between £2 and £4 (see figure 3).

In Britain it is not usual to rock-climb whilst wearing a rucksack since nearly all of our climbs have easy ways down, and it is so much simpler to leave the sack at the bottom of the cliff and pick it up later. Because of this a specially designed climbing sack is not really of first importance – indeed, I know of one very good climber who turns up at local outcrops carrying an ordinary grip. This causes looks of scorn and pity – until he proceeds to waltz up all the hard climbs!

Wherever a walk to the cliff is involved then some form of rucksack is necessary, the main consideration being that it should be strong, and an old army great pack is as good as anything.

Of course, there will come a time when a proper rucksack becomes essential. Many of the Scottish climbs, for example, involve carrying a sack simply because it would be awkward to go back to the foot of the crag to pick it up, or perhaps the climb is so long that it would be unwise from the point of view of weather and food, to be parted from your rucksack.

The framed rucksacks which are excellent for walking and camping holidays are a positive nuisance when climbing rocks. The frame catches against the rock and against the rope and there is a feeling of unbalance. On the other hand the small 'day' sack, as it is called, is not capacious enough to carry the food and gear for a weekend's expedition.

The compromise achieved by most climbers is to buy an alpine rucksack. This is large enough to hold everything necessary and yet neat enough to climb with.

Such a rucksack should be fairly tall but narrow, with a high centre of gravity when packed. It should be made of stout canvas, with a reinforced base, and preferably contain a bivvy sheet. The shoulder straps should be comfortable and adjustable. The top flap should be large enough to keep out the weather no matter how full the sack may be, and there should be no side pockets, since these snag against the rock. A metal hauling ring is useful.

The B.B. Snowcap and the Whillan's Alpinist are two popular rucksacks which are admirable for the climber, though there are others. The cost of such a sack is about £7.

2 Rock for Climbing

Rocks are the bare bones of the Earth; the skeleton which shows through wherever the thin flesh of grass and soil has been worn away by erosion. This erosion takes place more easily when the land is subjected to extreme and constant forces of wind and water, and so the rock shows through mostly on high hills and sea coasts. But rivers can play their part, too, and form precipitous gorges like that of the Avon at Bristol, and of course Man himself can lend a hand by excavating huge quarries. The rock which is exposed by all these means is often steep and challenging. Rock-climbing is the acceptance of that challenge.

Sometimes the challenge can turn out to be only a slight one, so that to overcome it all you need do is put one foot in front of the other, and keep a cool head, with perhaps an occasional steadying handhold or a pull up some awkward little step. The great crag of Pavey Ark, in the Lake District, can be overcome in this manner by following a curious ledge called Jack's Rake and this borderland between walking and rock-climbing is called scrambling, as we shall see in a moment. More often, however, the challenge of a crag looks formidable, if not impossible.

There is an old saying among rock-climbers that you should never judge the difficulty of a crag until you have rubbed noses with it. What at first appears to be smooth walls of rock reveals ledges and cracks when it is examined closer and it becomes possible to trace out with your mind's eye a line from one ledge to another, right from the bottom to the top. If such a line proves climbable it is said to 'go'.

Some of the features are common to all crags, and these are widely recognised and named by climbers, so that other climbers will know what they are talking about without too much bother. The most obvious of these are the big gullies;

deep, wide fissures cleaving into the crag and often containing a stream or waterfall. Just because they are such obvious chinks in the crag's defences, they were the favourite climbs of the early pioneers, but they are less popular nowadays. For one thing they give a rather hefty sort of climbing, they are frequently wet, and they are a natural chute for any falling stones. Nevertheless they are by no means always easy climbs and some of them are still worth climbing: Moss Ghyll, Scafell and Great Gully, Craig yr Ysfa, are two popular gully climbs.

Between the gullies a crag thrusts out in bold buttresses or sometimes sharp-backed ridges (arêtes) and it is on the open faces of these that most of the climbs will lie. If the buttress or ridge is well defined there will generally be one major route up it, taking the most obvious line, and several variants, which are usually harder. A typical example of this is Bowfell Buttress in the Lake District which has an original climb directly up its front and eleven alternatives on either hand.

Rifts in the crags which are too small to be called gullies are known as chimneys. They are usually slots wide enough to admit your whole body, but often too, they are little more than V-angle grooves. They can be any length, either forming just one part of a climb, like Slingsby's Chimney on Scafell Pinnacle, or a whole climb in themselves like the 200 ft Rake End Chimney on Pavey Ark.

Fissures which are so narrow that they will admit only an arm or leg, and sometimes not even that, are simply called cracks. Crack climbing is very important; it is the improvement in crack climbing which has helped to push up the modern standards of the sport.

Cracks, of course, can be horizontal and diagonal as well as vertical, and they can even prise away a layer of rock from the parent crag to make a flake – the most famous of which is the Great Flake on Scafell Central Buttress; a tremendous wedge of rock, and a hard climb.

Cracks, chimneys and even gullies often contain jammed blocks called chockstones. The larger ones can be awkward to climb over – they frequently form overhangs – but the smaller ones can be useful for a method of protection known

Figure 4
A STEEP WALL. The climber is ascending a steep wall at Stanage.
Notice the good holds and the fact that he is not being pulled by the
rope.

as the running belay, as we shall discover later: there have
even been cases of climbers inserting their own chockstones
on particularly difficult climbs.

Quite apart from the various cracks, the rock faces themselves form easily recognisable features. The sharp ridges
have been mentioned already, then there are the flat sloping
slabs, of which the most famous are the Idwal Slabs in
Snowdonia; almost 400 ft of uniform slope. Steeper – over
75° – flat areas are called walls, and these may even lean out

26

appreciably like the great limestone wall of Raven's Tor in Miller's Dale, Derbyshire. Where the rock juts out altogether it forms an overhang, and is likely to be difficult to negotiate because it tends to throw the climber off balance. Two exceptional overhangs – roofs, in fact – can be seen at Kilnsey Crag in Yorkshire and the Roches in the Peak District.

Until fairly recently climbers were rather particular about what sort of rock they climbed. They insisted that it should be rough, solid and sound, so that they could concentrate all their attention on the techniques of overcoming gravity. This has changed today; a modern climber will tackle any sort of rock if only to prove that it *is* climbable and routes have been made even on the desperately loose shale face of Mam Tor in Derbyshire and the polished slate of the Llanberis quarries, though it must be confessed that these are extremes which do not appeal to many.

The chief rocks enjoyed by climbers are the various hard and ancient rocks of the principal mountain areas like the Lake District and Wales, limestone, gritstone and to a lesser extent, sandstone. Each of these rocks has its own characteristics.

In the mountains, rocks like gneiss and porphyry offer splendid firmness and a rough texture with plenty of incut holds. Granite, too, is another crystalline rock which is good for climbing upon, though sometimes fine-grained granite has a decided lack of holds – such as the rock in Arran, for example. In Skye the rock is mainly gabbro, which is just about the firmest and roughest of all, with tremendous friction, though there is also plenty of basalt, a black, shiny rock which is frequently loose.

Outside the principal mountain areas the chief rock is certainly limestone. It outcrops in many parts of the country. Because of its steepness and looseness it has only recently become popular, and at first climbers used a lot of metal pegs (pitons) for protection, but gradually, as they came to know the material, they found it was not as terrible as they feared. It does demand good technique, however; holds can be very small and polished, the exposure (i.e. the sheer drop) is extreme, and the soundness of the rock is never entirely above suspicion. It can be very slippery in the rain.

Gritstone is just the opposite in many ways. Except in some of the gritstone quarries it is very sound and rough and rain makes little difference to its friction on boots. Because of this, 'holdless' cracks can be climbed and even the smallest wrinkles used as holds. Friction is everything on gritstone, with incut holds at a minimum, and since it is usually steep it gives very good practice in balance. Gritstone occurs in the Pennines within an area roughly bounded by Harrogate and Derby, north and south, Bolton and Sheffield, west and east. It is the rock upon which most of England's leading climbers served their apprenticeship.

Sandstone is similar to gritstone in that it has small rounded holds and good friction, but it is somewhat less reliable. There are big sandstone cliffs in the north of Scotland, but surprisingly little elsewhere. However, the small outcrops of the Kent-Sussex border are sandstone and they have special importance because they are the nearest rock-climbing to London.

In the last century, when climbing was a very new pastime, rock-climbers often referred to themselves as 'scramblers', but before many years had passed the climbs became so technically difficult that it was quite obvious they were more than mere scramblers.

Actually the differences between the harder scrambles and the easier rock-climbs are very slight, and one merges into the other. The main differences are that on a scramble you can halt almost anywhere, there are frequent large ledges, and you need to use your hands only intermittently. On a rock-climb hands are constantly in use and you can only take a rest at certain intervals, where the steep rock gives way to a ledge or stance.

All mountain walkers indulge in a bit of scrambling from time to time, but this does not make them into rock-climbers. To take an example: a really splendid fell-walk is that which climbs Bowfell in the Lake District by way of the Crinkle Crags ridge. It involves a tiny but exciting

Figure 5
THE BLACK ROCKS OF CROMFORD. One of the best known of the
Derbyshire gritstone outcrops. There are outcrops in many parts of
Britain – though not often as fine as this one.

scramble known as 'the bad step', which is really a little
chimney, and which would not be out of place on an easy
rock-climb. But as it is, it is isolated; there is no continuity of
difficulty, and so it can be regarded as a scramble. On the
other hand, if you climb Bowfell by its great buttress, you
find one difficulty after another, and so the buttress route
is a rock-climb.

Scrambling is an excellent introduction to real rock-
climbing. It teaches you the feel of rock, and that is very
important, it also demands a certain sense of rhythmical
balance, and some scrambles are very exposed. Even if you
learn your real rock-climbing on the local outcrops, it is a
good idea to spend the first few days when you visit the
mountains in doing some of the famous scrambles. Not
only do they provide grand mountain adventures but they
also give you some idea of the differences which length of
climb and changing weather can make between the outcrops
and the bigger hills.

29

Bearing in mind that more accidents happen to walkers and scramblers than to rock-climbers, you would be prudent to have an experienced climber as your companion for your first scrambles, especially if they include any of the more tricky routes. A high and narrow ridge can be an unnerving place when you are not accustomed to it, and having a friend along makes all the difference.

Any of the scrambles listed below makes a fine expedition. Choose a good day in summer, start early, and try to maintain a steady rate, resting only every hour or so. When you do rest, make it worthwhile – take fifteen or twenty minutes, remove your rucksack and nibble some chocolate. This way you will find your energy lasting throughout the day and the whole expedition will become more enjoyable as a result.

The easier scrambles will present very little difficulty but sooner or later you are bound to come up to one of the notorious 'bad bits' like the one on Crinkle Crags I mentioned just now. Examine it carefully and work out exactly how you are going to tackle it. Do not 'rush' it and do not panic. Remember that thousands of people have crossed it before you, so it can't be all that bad! If at first you don't succeed, as the saying goes, try and try again. You will probably find that each time you get a little further. But if in the end you simply cannot do it then you must retreat; some bad bits need considerable determination and there is no need to feel ashamed at failure. 'Pushing it', as climbers say when they mean someone is climbing beyond his skill, is foolish and dangerous.

In winter, many scrambles become serious mountaineering expeditions, especially in Scotland where the ice and snow can linger on into May. I have even had to use an ice-axe on the Crib Goch ridge of Snowdon as late as Easter. When conditions are like this the fell-walker and rock-climber must give way to the all-round competent mountaineer.

Here are some of the famous scrambles which are well worth doing. I have divided them into two groups, those of the first group being rather easier than those of the second. There are, of course, many more scrambles besides these, especially in Scotland.

The Stiperstone Pinnacles, Shropshire

Start from Plox Green. A fascinating scramble across a unique moor. Some of the pinnacles are difficult, but they can all be avoided if need be.

Traverse of Cnict, Snowdonia

Start from Croesor. Another curious hill – the 'Matterhorn of Wales' as locals call it.

Striding Edge, Helvellyn, Lake District

Start from Patterdale. One of the most famous scrambles in the country and very popular. Combined with a descent of Swirrel Edge, it makes a fine day out.

Sharp Edge, Blencathra, Lake District

Start from Scales. The scrambling is much shorter than the better known Striding Edge, but rather more difficult.

The Snowdon Horseshoe, Snowdonia

Start from the new Youth Hostel at Pen y Pass. The route goes via Crib Goch and Crib y Ddysgl to Snowdon and returns via the Lliwedd ridge. The finest mountain circuit south of the Scottish border.

Carn Mor Dearg Ridge, Ben Nevis, Scotland

Start from Fort William. From the summit of Ben Nevis the mountain falls away into a narrow ridge connecting it with Carn Mor Dearg across the head of the Allt a Mhuillin glen. Not technically difficult but the way down the ridge is hard to find in mist – there have been many accidents here. A good day is essential, and an early start.

The following routes all involve some easy rock-climbing

though only for short·stretches at a time. A rope is useful, and essential on the Scottish scrambles.

Jack's Rake, Pavey Ark, Lake District

Start from the New Dungeon Ghyll Hotel, Langdale. Not hard, but exposed near the top.

Traverse of Tryfan and the Glyders, Snowdonia

Start from Llyn Ogwen. Over the north ridge of Tryfan to Bwlch Tryfan then up Bristly Ridge to the summit of Glyder Fach. Descent by the Gribin Ridge. A fairly long day with lots of scrambling.

Aonach Eagach, Glencoe, Scotland

Start from The Meeting of Three Waters. A long ridge which runs from Am Bodach to Sgorr nam Fiannaidh and involves crossing some exposed pinnacles. The descent to Clachaig is dangerous in mist or darkness. Choose a fine summer's day.

Traverse of the Main Ridge, Arran

Start from Brodick. A long day and a magnificent expedition, but only to be undertaken with a very experienced companion. The A'Chir section of the ridge requires the use of a rope.

The Cuillins, Skye

The Cuillins are a complex of jagged ridges which offer the finest scrambling in Britain, but there are also considerable stretches of genuine rock-climbing involved. Should only be attempted with an experienced companion, who knows the area.

3 Balance Climbing

The first aim of any beginner at rock-climbing should be to achieve a good balance on small holds. There are two parts to this seemingly simple operation – first, to maintain balance whilst standing still and second, to maintain the balance whilst moving from one hold to the next.

Slabs are good for this sort of work. They give fairly uncomplicated climbing (though not always easy) at a steady angle, and if they are short then a lot of useful balance practice can be managed in two or three hours. Slabs on some of the smaller outcrops, especially gritstone, are ideal. The point is that they allow you to concentrate on the climbing without having to worry much about rope-work as you would need to do on a longer climb. In fact, short slabs need not be led at all – a friend, belayed at the top of the slab, can drop a rope down to you, and provided you know how to tie on properly and he knows how to take in the rope, nothing else is required. This is known as 'top roping' and is frequently used in instructing beginners.

Gritstone is particularly good for learning how to balance because the holds are often small and rounded, making it impossible to heave yourself up by brute force. Either you balance properly – or you fall off! The secret in this case lies in the tremendous frictional quality of the rock, which allows you to use minute wrinkles.

Let us imagine that you are standing at the foot of a gritstone slab, ready to make your first attempt at rock-climbing. Your instructor has tied you securely on to the end of a rope, which he begins to take in. 'OK!' he shouts, 'Start climbing!'

The slab slopes upwards at sixty degrees or so, smooth except for the worn looking little knobs and wrinkles which have obviously been used by thousands of your predecessors.

Hoping for the best, you reach for one hold and step up on another. Immediately, everything seems very much steeper! The rock seems to stretch limitlessly up and you have an urgent desire to reach the top as quickly as possible. Like a madman you scrabble up from hold to hold, in a desperate race against gravity. After what seems ages, but is probably no more than two or three minutes, you lie panting on the top. You've made it! 'Well,' remarks the instructor, 'at least you got up, which is something, I suppose. Now go down to the start again, and this time try to *climb* it!'

This time you know what to expect. You realise that the holds are sufficient – just – but that they must be used in a certain order. You are starting to think less about size of holds and more about sequence and you have taken your first important step on the way to becoming a climber.

Figure 6a (*left*)

BALANCE. A typical gritstone slab. Notice the position of the body, hands held low, and heels down. He is in perfect stationary balance – he is not actually holding anything, merely touching the rock.

Figure 6b (*centre*)

BALANCE ON A STEEP SLAB. A winter day on Yorkshire limestone. The climbing is on tiny holds – about Severe in standard.

Figure 6c (*right*)

BALANCE ON A SIDEWAYS MOVE. Notice how the climber is using pressure holds. The move is Hard Severe – but only a few feet from the ground.

Even before you leave the ground you figure out the first few moves. Then you step up boldly and move smoothly from hold to hold, not by leaps and bounds – sometimes you may step up no more than two or three inches.

Three important facts quickly become apparent:

1. Balance is much easier if you hold your body away from the rock: only fingers and toes should be touching.
2. It is less tiring to keep your arms about shoulder height as much as possible, and let your weight come onto your feet.
3. Stationary balance is easier if you press your heels down, and continual standing on tip-toe results in leg-shake, which is not at all pleasant.

One important aspect of balance climbing which will not

be obvious at first is the need to maintain three point contact with the rock. By this I mean that of your four limbs, three should always be attached to the rock whilst you move the remaining one. In other words, move *either* one arm *or* one leg at a time, never both together. This requires constant and definite practice; it will make your climbing both neater and safer. Study the climbers in figure 6.

A few slab climbs of this sort and you will begin to realise that holds come in all shapes and sizes. Some offer no actual grip yet are useful to press upon whilst others are distinctly square cut and offer more leverage. Best of all are those your fingers can curl over for a pull because they are incut – the big ones of this sort are called 'jugs' (from jug-handles) and where one occurs just as things are getting pretty desperate it is known as a Thank God hold – you may guess why!

Sometimes the only way up is to use a flat pressure hold set at chest height – there is just such a situation on a well-known little slab at Cromford Black Rocks. It is impossible to step up, obviously, and you are forced to resort to a delicate procedure known as a *mantelshelf*. You place the palms of your hands flat on the hold and then do a press-up until you can place your foot on the same hold. Keeping in balance all the time you then have to straighten up. On the easier grade of climb mantelshelves usually have big ledges, but on harder climbs they can be very delicate affairs – there are even one-handed mantelshelves (figure 7).

Not all the useful holds are horizontal. Some slope awkwardly, and others can only be used sideways for steadying pulls, or perhaps to press your feet against. Then too, there are pinch-grips, little knobs which can be squeezed between finger and thumb and there are even holds which are undercut, but useful for maintaining balance.

The size, nature and spacing of the holds determine the difficulty of a climb. A slab which has plenty of incut holds will obviously be easier than one which has only a few pressure holds because the *moves* are more difficult in the second case. Incidentally, you can have too much of a good thing – a climb which has nothing but enormous jugs all the

Figure 7*a* (*left*)
A MANTELSHELF MOVE. The climber now has to put one foot where
his hands are and balance up on it.
Figure 7*b* (*right*)
A MANTELSHELF MOVE. Climbs sometimes finish with a mantelshelf.

way up is seldom satisfactory because it is too easy; you
may as well climb the wall bars of your school gym.

It was the great pioneer climber, Owen Glynne Jones,
who first proposed a sensible system for grading climbs
according to their difficulty. Jones' system was modified
as time went on, and it now stands as follows, in ascending
order of difficulty:

Easy, Moderate, Difficult, Very Difficult, Severe, Very
Severe and Extremely Severe.

From this you can see that a climb which is described as
'Very Difficult' in a guide-book is in fact only half way up
the scale, and there are three harder grades. This has come

about because since the pioneering days increasingly difficult climbs have been mastered and new grades have been invented to fit them. By today's high standards, 'V.Diff.' as it is commonly called, is regarded as the end of the elementary stage, no more.

The system has been made more flexible by using the prefixes Hard and Mild. For example, in the Langdale guide-book we read that a climb on Gimmer Crag, called Bracket and Slab, is Mild Severe in standard, which means that though it is definitely harder than V.Diff. it only just makes the higher grade. On the same crag a climb called Dipthong is graded Hard Severe because though not reaching Very Severe standard it is somewhat harder than one would expect on an ordinary Severe climb.

Gradings take into account the hardest pitch on a climb and a good climb is one which keeps close to its grade all the way. Occasionally, other factors influence the grading of a climb. If, for example, a climb is very exposed and has poor protection it gains a serious nature which the guide-book writer might reflect by giving it a high grading. One famous instance of this is a classic route called Main Wall on Cyrn Las in Wales, which is graded as Hard Severe though it might not be technically quite up to that standard. On the other hand a short boulder problem of fifteen to twenty feet might be downgraded slightly or described as 'technically Very Severe'.

The system works well on the whole and you will soon get the hang of it. At the same time it is not infallible – guide-book compilers are only human, and what one expert considers to be Mild V.S. another might grade as Hard Severe and vice versa. Sometimes, too, climbs change with time and usage. On Carreg Wastad in Wales a climb called The Wrinkle came down from Severe to V.Diff. whilst another called Crackstone Rib did just the reverse. On Tryfan, the climb known as Soap Gut came down from Very Severe to Very Difficult! Such changes are not very common but it is prudent, when visiting a crag for the first time, to try a climb which is well within your powers first, just to see how standards compare. This is especially the case on the outcrops where climbs are usually well up to standard.

On the sandstone outcrops of southern England a numerical system of I to VI, in ascending order is used, but this method of classification has found little favour elsewhere.

If you begin your climbing on short slab pitches, as suggested, you will probably find yourself tackling Diff. and V.Diff. grades almost immediately. There is no need to be alarmed about this: you will be well protected by the top rope and will come to no harm. You will learn much more about balance climbing than you would from long, uninteresting Moderates with huge jugs.

Even some of the outcrop Severes are not beyond the scope of a novice, provided he is firmly held from above – Plate Glass Slab at Stanage and Railway Slab at the Black Rocks of Cromford, for example; two excellent balance climbs.

The outcrops are full of marvellous little slabs like those just mentioned, but in the real mountains you will have to search for the sort of thing you require. Good training slabs are not often found on popular crags, and when they are, as with Brown Slabs on Shepherd's Crag in Borrowdale, they tend to be crowded. The best idea is to glean through the guide-books for obscure little crags where you can practice in peace. There are quite a few up Combe Ghyll in the Lake District, and in Wales I have found Little Tryfan and Craig y Aderyn very useful.

If climbs consisted of nothing else but slabs they would soon become rather boring, but fortunately this is far from being the case. Cracks of various widths have to be climbed also.

The widest cracks are known as chimneys, and the manner of climbing them depends very much on their actual width. If possible the back or one of the sides of the chimney is treated as a slab or a wall because this is the simplest, but all too often the chimney is too narrow or smooth for this.

A wide chimney is best climbed by the technique called bridging or straddling. In this you place one foot on either wall using handholds either on the walls or the back of the chimney. You move up accordingly, and the result is often elegant and untiring. It is a popular method, and one which

can also be used on some V-grooves and corners (figure 8*a*).

For narrower chimneys the backing-up method is employed in which you place your back against one wall of the chimney and your knees or feet against the other. Progress is made by moving up your feet and back alternately, and no definite holds are required since you are kept in position by pressure and friction. To do it properly with a minimum of effort is not always easy and a little foresight helps (figure 8*b*).

The first consideration is to work out which way to face, left or right. Sometimes the guide-book will tell you and if it does be sure to follow the instructions for it usually means that facing the other way is very awkward, but often you have to work it out for yourself from the look of the thing. Pulling out of the chimney, at the top, can sometimes be awkward.

A useful tip, too, is to push the knot of your rope round

40

Figure 8a (*left*)
A Bridging Move
Figure 8b (*centre*)
Backing-up a Chimney
Figure 8c (*right*)
A Narrow Chimney. This chimney is too narrow for the techniques in 8a and 8b.

to the front so that it does not make a painful lump in your back as you press against the chimney. You must also try to maintain a steady position – it is amazingly easy for your feet to work up too high; there is a well known climbing film showing a girl beginner doing just this very thing until she is almost upside-down!

You have also to work out just how far inside the chimney you should go. The natural reaction is to squeeze inside as far as you can, but this is not always a good thing – sometimes better progress can be made near the outer edges.

Some chimneys are so narrow that even backing-up becomes impossible. The method employed then is to jam your body in and wriggle or 'thrutch' up using friction and whatever holds are available. Here again it is sometimes better not to jam yourself too tightly in the chimney if there is a possibility of good holds on the outer edges (figure 8c).

Long chimneys which are climbed by thrutching are

always tiring, though fortunately they are usually so tight that you can let go of the rock altogether without falling off. Two well known chimneys which are extraordinary thrutches are the Moderate, Fat Man's Chimney at Cromford, and Intermediate Gully, on Dow Crag, Coniston, which is Severe.

Chimneys and gullies are often blocked by enormous jammed boulders known as chockstones and in a gully they can be so big as to form a sort of cave. Sometimes you can climb between the boulder and the back of the chimney – a through route, as it is called, like the spectacular through route on Ivy Chimney, Milestone Buttress in Wales. Usually, however, the only way past a chockstone is to bridge or back and knee past it.

One of the unpleasant features of gullies and chimneys is that some of them have piles of loose stones on their ledges and chockstones and it is only too easy for a careless leader to shower these down on his unfortunate companions.

I have put gullies and chimneys together because they have many common features. On the whole the climbing is strenuous, and it can be rather dirty and wet. Such climbs are not popular today, as you can imagine, but there are a few routes still worth doing. Among the easier ones you might like to try are Great Gully and Rake End Chimney, on Pavey Ark, Langdale, or Ivy Chimney just mentioned, or Flake Chimney on Dinas Bach in the Llanberis Pass. More difficult routes include such famous classics as Moss Ghyll, Scafell; Great Gully, Craig yr Ysfa; Great Gully, Cyrn Las and Clachaig Gully in Glencoe. Some of the Scottish gullies are formidable canyons worth visiting for the rock scenery alone.

Now and again you come across a chimney which is a bit of a freak. Perhaps the most celebrated is the Doves Nest in Borrowdale, which is a whole complex of chimneys formed underground by some enormous landslip. The climbing is fairly easy, though you need a good torch. It is more like caving than climbing, but interesting enough to be worth a visit. In Wales the only comparable thing is much less enclosed – Lockwood's Chimney.

There are even horizontal chimneys which can be crossed

by simply crawling or squirming along them; a process known as a stomach traverse. One of the longest of these crosses the face of the massive Plum Buttress in Derbyshire, and though a traverse across it is sensational, it could hardly be called climbing!

When a fissure is too narrow to admit your body it is simply called a crack. Cracks play a part in almost every climb and it is the development of crack-climbing which has contributed as much as anything else to the present high standard of the sport in Britain.

The easier cracks are ragged edged and give magnificent holds so that they can be climbed in the same way as a slab, but many cracks need at least a few moves which rely upon pure friction. The technique for this is known as jamming.

On wider cracks simple boot jamming is generally all that is needed. To do this you jam your boot in the crack and push up on it, then jam your other boot higher and so on. Sometimes only the boot toe can be got into the crack, but this might well be enough to provide the necessary friction. Turning your foot sideways can be a help on narrow cracks and it is in situations like this that the special rock-climbing boots such as PA's, which I will mention later, are of great assistance. Whatever you do, you must try not to make the jam *too* effective, or you will find yourself stuck. I was once on a climb where the second got his boot so firmly stuck that he had to unlace it and take his foot out, then prise the boot free!

Foot jams are usually not difficult, but hand jams need some mastering. If the crack is fairly wide a good arm jam might be possible but otherwise, for cracks which have no normal holds, two main types of hand jam are employed.

The first might be called the fist jam: your loosely clenched fist is pushed into the crack and then clenched harder. This has the effect of pushing out the sides of your fist and jamming it in the crack. You then pull up on your clenched fist.

The true hand jam, however, is different. In this you put your hand sideways into the crack and then push your thumb hard across the palm – if you try it right now you will appreciate at once how it jams in a crack. Such a jam is

Figure 9a (*left*)

CRACK CLIMBING. The climber is pulling up on a chockstone. Notice how he has twisted his right foot to obtain a toe jam in the crack.

Figure 9b (*right*)

LAYBACK MOVE

a very effective hold; indeed, experts have claimed that they can hang from a hand jam for far longer than they could from even a good incut hold.

Until you learn to do them properly hand jams can be rather painful, but they are worth learning because on the harder climbs they are invaluable.

There are all sorts of variations possible on hand jams as you will find out from experience. It is even possible to pull up on finger jams.

Jamming is very important but there are other ways of climbing cracks, depending on their situation. For example, if the crack is not too steep you can use your hands in opposi-

44

tion on either edge of the crack; the counteracting forces will keep you in balance. On corner cracks the layback method can be used, where you pull on the crack with your hands and at the same time with your feet press against the opposite corner (figure 9*b*). You need to be sure that your hands and feet are not too wide apart or you will slip out of position and fall off, and you also need to move quickly before the strength in your arms gives out. In fact, laybacking is the most strenuous movement in climbing and it is avoided if some other method will suffice. Some of the outcrops have short, easy laybacks where you can try your skill, but you need to be something of an expert before you try some of the classics such as Altar Crack at Rivelin Edge, near Sheffield or the Flake Crack at Helsby in Cheshire.

Horizontal cracks are often used to change the line of a climb – for example, to avoid an overhang. Sometimes they provide a continuous foothold whilst your hands use holds on the wall above, or vice versa. Occasionally they are used for a hand traverse – that is where you must move sideways depending solely on your hands because there are no footholds.

A hand traverse can be very exhausting. Before starting on one it is as well to be sure you have it all worked out and that you have the strength to complete it. Retreat may not be possible. Fortunately perhaps, pure hand traverses, where there are absolutely no footholds, are fairly rare and generally very short. As you might expect, hand traverses are not common on the easier climbs: there is one on Corvus, Raven Crag, Borrowdale and also on Donkey's Ears, a popular climb on Shepherd's Crag in the same valley. In Wales there is a hand traverse near the top of the Milestone Buttress Ordinary Route. One of the longest and most strenuous hand traverses in the country is to be found on the Girdle Traverse of Grey Buttress, Anglezarke Quarry, near Bolton – about thirty feet without a rest!

Slab technique and crack technique form ninety-nine per cent of the climber's art. The rest – overhangs, arêtes and so on, can usually be overcome by applying the same basic principles and a dash of common-sense. There is, however, one rather strange technique which is sometimes employed in the

Figure 10
A HAND TRAVERSE. The climber is crossing the short hand traverse on Central Buttress, Cromford Black Rocks, a popular Very Difficult.

Alps but so far as I am aware is only used on one climb in Britain. This is a method of climbing a holdless ridge and is known as *à cheval* – literally, like riding a horse. The ridge must be at a fairly moderate angle and you sit astride it with your hands on the crest. Progress is made by a series of small frog-hops. It is not easy to do this properly because it feels most insecure, but if you wish to try it out you must journey to the Black Rocks of Cromford where the Stonnis Arête can be climbed *à cheval*.

4   The Main Rope

The art of climbing can be divided readily into two parts:

1. Those skills which enable us to overcome the problems set by the rock.
2. Those skills which ensure us maximum protection against a fall.

Chapter 3 outlined the first of these. The basis for the second part is competent ropework.

The use of a rope in climbing mystifies most outsiders. Some believe that climbers actually climb up the rope, like a super Indian rope-trick, whilst others think that the leader does the climb and then hauls everyone else up on the rope. In fact, the rope is not used for *climbing* at all, but for *protection*.

But, you will hear people ask, surely if everyone is roped together, if one falls he will pull the others off with him? It is a fair question and it *has* happened, mostly in the old days before proper rope techniques were worked out. The point of modern rope work is to protect the whole party, as we shall see.

Modern climbing ropes are manufactured in two different types, each with various thicknesses. The material for both kinds is nylon and the difference lies in the way the strands are put together. In Britain the traditional rope is hawser laid, where the nylon fibres are spun into strands and three of these strands are then twisted together to make a rope. The Continental method, which is becoming increasingly popular, is known as kernmantel and in this case long filaments of nylon run the entire length of the rope, without any twisting, and are held together by a braided outer sheath.

The standard thickness of rope recommended for rock-

climbing (as distinct from Alpine climbing) is No. 4 hawser
$1\frac{3}{8}''$ circ. or kernmantel 11 mm diam. For two climbers
120 ft is generally sufficient, though 150 ft is useful on some
of the harder climbs.

Here is a comparison of the two types:

	Hawser	*Kernmantel*
Weight (120 ft)	6.5 lbs	6.6 lbs
Breaking load	4,200 lbs	4,300 lbs
Extension	40% +	25% +
Cost (approx.)	£7 10s. 0d.	£8

The only significant difference, as you can see, is in the
extension, i.e. the amount the rope will stretch under load.
A large extension is important because it prevents the rope
from snapping under the impact of a shock load and it also
helps to reduce the body blow which a falling climber
receives. The figure quoted for kernmantel shows that it is
not as extensible as hawser laid rope, though a recent
British kernmantel rope is reported to be better.

There is little to choose between these two for your first
rope. The kernmantel handles more smoothly, is less liable
to kink than the hawser, and the outer sheath protects it
against abrasion. On the other hand the hawser has known
extensibility and keeps its knots better. Also it is possible
for the inner core of the kernmantel to be damaged whilst
the outer sheath remains whole – a serious fact which would
go unnoticed.

In recent years a number of climbers have taken to using
two thinner ropes instead of one thick one. The ropes
recommended for this are No. 3 hawser $1\frac{1}{4}''$ circ. or 9 mm
diam. kernmantel. Obviously this is safer still since it is
unlikely that two ropes would ever break simultaneously
and the shock loading on one would reduce the impact on
the second. Another advantage is that where the rope has to
run through a number of karabiners, the drag is reduced if
the two ropes are used alternately. Two separate ropes are
better than one long one doubled for this 'double rope
technique' as it is called.

The disadvantages, from the beginner's point of view,
outweigh the advantages. First, it is more expensive, but

apart from the cost, two ropes are much more difficult to handle in a proper manner. The system is excellent for skilled climbers but too cumbersome for a novice.

Other sizes of nylon rope are manufactured besides those already mentioned. They are all too weak to be used as a main rope on rock climbs, but they do have other uses in the mountains. Here is a list:

Hawser laid rope

No. 1. $\frac{5}{8}''$ circ. BS 1,000 lbs	Prusik loops.
No. 2. $\frac{7}{8}''$ circ. BS 2,000 lbs	Abseiling. Double for snow climbs. 'Emergency' rope for scrambling.
No. 3. $1\frac{1}{4}''$ circ. BS 3,500 lbs	Double for rock climbs. Single for snow climbs. Abseiling.
No. 4. $1\frac{3}{8}''$ circ. BS 4,200 lbs	Standard rope.

Kernmantel rope

9 mm diam. BS 3,200 lbs	As for No. 3 above. Good for artificial climbing.
11 mm diam. BS 4,300 lbs	Standard climbing rope.

This kernmantel is of British make (Viking); Continental kernmantel is obtainable in five thicknesses from 11 mm to 4 mm. It is excellent quality rope, but twice as expensive as the British.

Occasionally you may still see hemp rope being used for climbing – it was the standard rope before nylon came along. Hemp is in every way inferior: weaker, less flexible, difficult to handle when wet or frozen, and it rots. On the other hand, the only fault with nylon is that it has a low melting point – about 480°F, which can easily be reached by friction. For this reason nylon should never be allowed to run over nylon.

Nylon rope is expensive, but if it is cared for it will last for a long time. Keep it stored away from strong sunlight and chemicals which might affect its fibres, e.g. car battery acid and strong cleaning bleaches. In the case of hawser ropes watch out for sharp edges of rock which can damage the fibres and try not to stand on the rope, particularly if there are sharp stones on the ground.

It is common-sense to have a periodical inspection of your rope, foot by foot. If it is hawser laid look for cuts and notice how, in an old rope, the surface becomes furry due to the constant abrasion of fibres. With a kernmantel rope examine it to see whether the sheath is damaged. If there is serious damage to your rope it will have to be taken out of use, though if the damage is at one end a piece can be chopped off and you will still have a serviceable if somewhat shorter, rope. If the rope is good, but too short for climbing purposes after damage, it can be cut up into slings. The cut ends of a nylon rope can be sealed by melting them with a match.

For carrying purposes the rope is coiled bandolier fashion. An easy way of doing this is to sit down, place your left hand palm upwards on your left knee and coil the rope round from your left hand under your left boot and so on. This ensures that the loops are of equal length, and by a strange coincidence, they are always of just the right size for fitting across the shoulders of whoever does the coiling. The end of the rope is secured by whipping – turn back the original end by about a foot then whip the final end round this tightly and finish off by pushing it through the loop so formed and drawing the whole thing tight (see figure 11).

In Britain the usual climbing partnership consists of two people, the leader and his second. This is the most conven-ient number since there is the minimum of waiting and small stances can be used. If both climbers are of equal ability it is quicker still – they can lead through, or take alternate leads, which saves the time consumed on changing belays. On some climbs the stances are so small that this is

Figure 11
HOW TO TIE THE
KNOT ON A COILED
ROPE

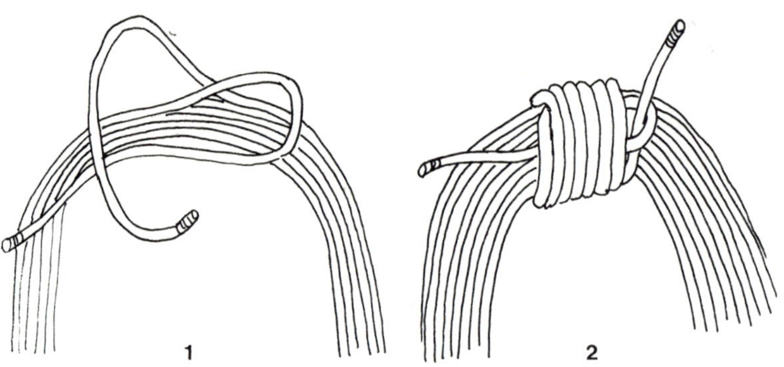

50

almost essential – Murray's Route on Dow Crag, for instance, or Cemetary Gates on Dinas Cromlech.

Nevertheless, though two is most convenient, it is not uncommon to see ropes of three (or even more), particularly on the easier climbs. It is usual to allow 120 ft or 150 ft of rope between each two members of a party: it is never a good policy to stint yourself on rope.

The simplest way of tying on the rope, and the one advisable for a beginner, is to take one end round your waist and fasten it into a loop by means of a bowline (figure 12a). To prevent the knot from coming undone it should be secured by two half hitches. The waistloop so formed should be comfortable but not slack – there should be no chance of it pulling up under your armpits. At the same time you need to be able to move the knot from side to side, so the loop must have some freedom.

The chief disadvantage of tying onto the main rope in this way is that in the event of a fall, all the strain comes onto a single thickness of rope and such concentrated force could injure the climber internally. However, as you will be climbing as a second man and not a leader, this hardly applies and so you can use it with confidence. As you will see later, leaders often use other means of tying on, but never forget that in the event of an emergency there may come a time when you need to know the direct method.

In fact, this applies to all the methods described in this chapter: they are basic, and though various devices have been invented to make them safer or easier you must first of all learn how to climb without them. Some day the need may arise when you are forced to rely on nothing but the rope.

Let us imagine that the moment has arrived for you to begin your first long climb. You have already managed a number of short outcrop climbs and you know all about balance, and chimneys and such like. Perhaps you have even managed to top-rope a Severe! It comes as something of a disappointment to learn that your first 'big' climb is to be no harder than a modest Difficult.

The reason for this is really quite simple. Though you may have proved yourself capable of performing all sorts

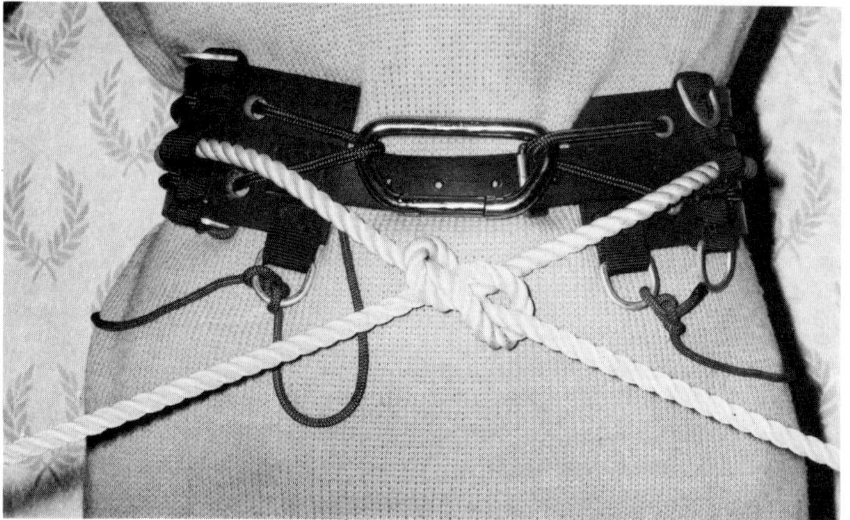

of hard gymnastics on rock, you know nothing about rope handling. The time has arrived to learn the art of *protection*, and you need a climb which is easy enough not to worry you, so that you can concentrate on the rope-work.

Best for this is a longish climb of Difficult or perhaps one of the easier Very Difficults, where there is little exposure, the stances are good and the belays sound. Tryfan is a good mountain for this: Milestone Ordinary, North Buttress and Pinnacle Rib are all good and so is Ampitheatre Buttress on Craig yr Ysfa, though a little harder. In the Lake District there are the climbs on Scout Crag in Langdale, the easier ridges of Gable and C Buttress on Dow Crag, among others.

Figure 12a (*left*)
THE BOWLINE WAIST TIE
Figure 12b (*right*)
THE TARBUCK METHOD. A generous loop is left between the krab and the Tarbuck knot. A better method for tying the waist-length is a fisherman's knot and half-hitches.
Figure 12c (*bottom left*)
A CLIMBING HARNESS

Taking the coil of rope from your shoulders, you first *uncoil it completely*. This is the only certain way of ensuring that it will run freely, and there is nothing so annoying to a leader as being told to 'hang on a bit' whilst his second untangles the knitting.

When you are satisfied that the rope will run freely, you each tie onto an end and the leader starts climbing. You, as the second, have two jobs to do:

1. See that the rope runs out smoothly.
2. Watch closely the line taken by the leader so that when your turn comes you will not need to waste time fumbling around, wondering which way to go.

53

The leader climbs up until he reaches a good ledge where there are belay points — that is, something to which he can tie himself whilst he brings you up. The distance he has climbed is known as a pitch, and it may be anything from twenty to a hundred feet; only very rarely is it more or less than this. If the pitch is short and easy — as for example at the start of Milestone Ordinary — he may decide to push on through the next pitch as well, to save time, in which case you will need to keep a keen eye on the rope to see that he does not run short. When there is only ten or fifteen feet of rope left it is usual to warn your leader of the fact so that he can look for a belay.

When he is ready to bring you up a sequence of commands comes into operation:

Leader: 'Taking in the slack!' *He pulls in all the spare rope and when the tug reaches you —*
Second: 'That's me!'
Leader: 'Climb when you're ready!'
Second: *When you are ready* 'Climbing!' *and you start to climb.*

Experienced climbers often modify these commands when they know their partner well. The important point is that communication should be sharp and clear — you may be out of one another's sight, and it is important that each should know exactly what the other is doing. There are three or four other calls recognised by climbers—
'Slack!' Means stop pulling, let me have more rope.
'Take in!' Means take the rope in faster.
'Tight rope!' A warning that you are finding the moves hard and feel you might come off. Whenever a fall is likely a warning shout should be given if possible.
'Below!' A general warning given whenever you accidentally kick down a loose stone or drop something — there may be other climbers below.

If your leader is a good chap, with some faith in your ability, you will find as you climb that he takes the rope in so smoothly that you scarcely know it is there. A bad leader will let it hang loose so that it gets in your way, and this is dangerous too because if you slip you will have further to fall and it will be more difficult to arrest the rope. Almost as bad is the chap who insists on hauling you up every pitch like a sack of potatoes!

When you reach your leader's stance you will see that whatever had happened you could not have pulled him off the cliff because he has taken the precaution of tying himself to some solid object such as a spike of rock or a tree. This is called a static belay or anchor.

To make a static belay with the main rope simply take a length of the rope as it comes from your waist, pass it around your belay point and bring it back to your waist loop. It is then fastened by means of two half hitches (figure 13*a*).

There are a number of points to watch. First, remember that the purpose of the static belay is to prevent whoever is using it from being pulled from his stance, and so it should be able to withstand a sudden jerk *in the right direction*. Many spikes look good but are useless because the rope would ride off under strain. Quite often the temptation is to use a large but wrongly placed spike when a smaller, better placed one would be more appropriate. There is even a case for using two belays, if any single one is doubtful, and in extreme cases a piton may have to be used.

If you have a choice of belays, and often you have on the easier climbs, then choose one which is as high above the stance as conveniently possible, or, alternatively, use a lower belay point sitting down – the aim in both cases being to have the belay loop already in tension, not slack.

The soundest type of anchor is a thread, taken round a tree or chockstone. Obviously it cannot ride off, but care is needed to ensure that the tree or chockstone is sound.

When you join your leader at his stance it is now your turn to fix a belay, and you do this *before* he takes his off. There should never be a moment on any stance where both partners are without belays – the dangers are obvious.

When he is satisfied that your belay is sound the leader begins the next pitch. Once again you have to pay out the rope smoothly, but this time with a difference – you pay it out using a dynamic belay.

The point here is that your leader is now a considerable distance above the ground and should he fall it is your responsibility to arrest that fall as soon as possible. You

Figure 13*b*
SLING AND KRAB BELAY

Figure 13*c*
WAIST BELAY

Figure 13*a*
BELAY USING THE MAIN ROPE

must obviously be in a position to control the rope.

This is achieved by paying out the rope around your waist as shown in figure 13c. Your waist now acts like a brake drum, with considerable friction between it and the rope and by bringing your arms together the friction is increased. Using this method, your chances of holding a falling leader are greatly increased.

However, the waist belay is open to many abuses and frequently it is wrongly applied. The following points are very important:

1. Your directing hand (the one doing the paying out) should be the hand nearest to the leader.
2. Your other arm (the controlling arm) should have one twist of rope round it and be held close to your side.
3. You should pay out smoothly, watching your leader all the time, allowing him a few feet of slack but no more. The rope should be free to run – no knitting.
4. You should be fully aware of the direction any fall is likely to take, and pay particular attention to runners, about which I shall have more to say later.

Above all, alertness is the key to good belaying. Never mind what the bloke on the next climb is doing, or how beautiful the scenery is: keep your mind on the job in hand!

Although the waist belay is the best method yet devised for holding a falling leader, it is not perfect, and the unpleasant truth of the matter is that if the leader falls you are in for a shock, both physically and mentally. Unless the rope is properly controlled it runs out at incredible speed, and you will receive severe rope burns on your hands. If the rope runs out completely you will be jerked onto your static belay with a stunning impact. When a leader has a serious fall, the second suffers too.

Belaying gloves help to prevent hand burns. Special gloves can be bought for this purpose, but really any old pair of leather gloves will suffice, the tougher they are, the better. The dangers of climbing with bare arms or bare back should be fairly obvious.

The waist belay does not come naturally and needs plenty of practice to make it effective. You will sometimes see climbers using an older method called the shoulder belay where the rope is paid across one shoulder and under the other armpit, and in fact this is rather more comfortable, especially on small stances. However, it is not as safe as the waist belay – in fact the climber can be jerked upside down trying to arrest a fall.

I have deliberately chosen the belaying situation as it occurs at the first stance because this is where proper belaying usually begins. There are times, however, when you will need to belay the leader right from ground level:

1. Where the ground falls away steeply below the first pitch.
2. Where the leader uses runners on his first pitch.

At the end of every pitch the belaying procedure is repeated. You will see from this that at any time during the ascent, one climber is attached to the cliff, and so it should not be possible for the entire party to come to grief.

When the party consists of three or more, the same procedure is adopted. Only one man climbs at a time, so that in a rope of three people, two would always be belayed whilst one climbed. This is doubly safe, but obviously slower since each belay has to be repeated for the third man (figure 14).

All this may sound very complicated but in practice it is really quite simple, and essential for safety. Here is a brief outline of the sequence again:

Rope uncoiled. Tie on.
Leader climbs first pitch. Belays.
Second climbs first pitch. Belays.
Leader removes his belay. Climbs second pitch. Belays.
Second removes his belay. Climbs second pitch. Belays.
And so on until the ascent is completed.

Figure 14
Opposite page CAMPSITE CRACK, AGDEN EDGE. A rope of three tackling a popular Very Difficult climb. The second man is belayed at the top of the first pitch, whilst the leader climbs the v-groove above.

5 Extra Protection

In the last chapter you read about the use of the main rope in climbing, and I tried to show how it is possible to climb using nothing else by way of protection. It is an invaluable way of training on the easier climbs: there is no better way of learning how to handle a rope and how to belay properly and safely.

On your visits to the crags, however, you will soon discover that climbers have modified the original system to make full use of the modern materials such as nylon and chromolly steel. It is these which have largely been responsible for the modern conception of hard climbing. They allow the margin of safety to be drawn very fine.

The chief piece of equipment in all this is the steel snap-link or karabiner. 'Krabs' as they are often called, originated in the Eastern Alps quite some time ago, but the chief fault with the early models was that the mild steel used was not really strong enough. Even since they first appeared ways have been sought to make krabs stronger and too often the snap-link was also the weak link.

Perfection has still not been achieved, and one result of this is that there is a very wide variety of karabiners on the market. One catalogue alone lists fourteen.

Basically, the karabiner is a steel or alloy oval (see figure 15) about 10 cm long on one side of which there is a spring loaded catch or gate. When you press the gate the krab opens, allowing a rope or piton to be slipped onto the ring. When you release the gate, it springs shut. On some models there is a metal sleeve which can be screwed over the closed gate, locking it completely – this is known as a screwgate krab.

Sometimes the oval shape is varied – there are pear shaped and kidney shaped ones, for instance – but recent research has

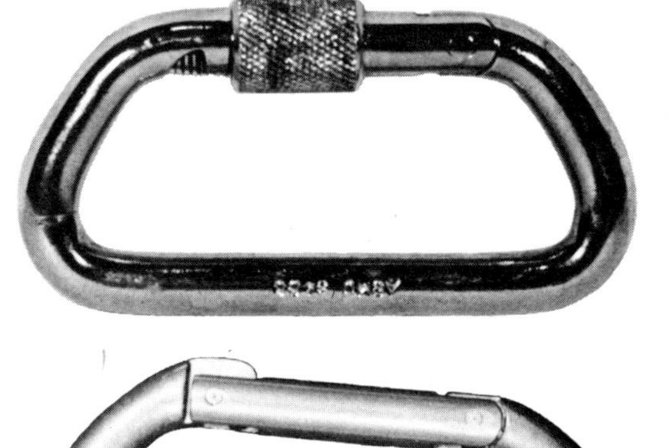

Figure 15*a*
THE ASMU SCREWGATE KARABINER.
The screw sleeve is in the 'open'
position. Recommended as the strongest
karabiner.
Figure 15*b*
THE ALLAIN ALLOY KARABINER.
A very strong krab, light in weight,
and useful for runners and artificial
climbing.

shown that the strongest are those shaped like a letter D, with the gate on the curved side. The straight side is the one which bears the load.

Like the rope itself, a krab might come under shock load at any time and so obviously it should be at least as strong as the rope. Because of this, international climbing associations have adopted a standard minimum breaking strain of 4,500 lbs (with the gate closed – a krab is much weaker when the gate is open). Curiously enough, a number of well-known karabiners do not reach this standard and so they should only be used in cases where there is to be no shock load – as for example in artificial climbing (more about this later) and sack hauling.

Improvements to karabiners are being made all the time but at the moment the strongest one available to the general public is the German ASMU type. This is made of chrome vanadium steel with a breaking strain of 7,500 lbs. No other krab comes anywhere near this for strength, and the vanadium steel is rust-proof as well.

Unfortunately, the price of the ASMU is high: 21s. for the ordinary krab or 25s. with screwgate. There is really no substitute but the best British equivalent is the Hiatt

(5,000 lbs) which costs about half as much. You will need about half-a-dozen krabs, and more later on in your career.

It pays to look after your karabiners, discarding any that are faulty. Screwgates need a drop of oil occasionally or they become stiff and oil can also be applied to the gate pin. You should examine the gate from time to time to see that it is still closing correctly: over a period of time the spring sometimes weakens or the gate gets out of true and does not close when it ought. Dropping a krab down a cliff can set up hidden fractures in the metal and any krab which has suffered in this way should be discarded or at least only used for light duty such as sack-hauling.

Screwgates have an advantage in that they prevent a karabiner from opening accidentally. Accidental opening can occur if the gate is pressed against an edge of rock or if another rope or karabiner presses down on it. The rope might jump out of the krab, possibly with serious consequences, but in any case an open karabiner is much weaker than a closed one.

On the other hand, a screwgate can be awkward to handle on steep rock and my own preference is to use a screwgate for waist tie, belaying and abseiling and ordinary krabs for runners and artificial climbing.

Using karabiners opens a whole new dimension in protection beginning with tying on. It makes possible the Tarbuck System invented by a Liverpool climber, Ken Tarbuck.

The system consists of a separate waist length to which the main rope is attached using a karabiner and the special Tarbuck knot (figure 12*b*). The waistlength is made of 25 ft of $\frac{3}{4}''$ hemp which can be wound round your waist to form a sort of multiple rope belt. The ends are tied together with a reef knot and half hitches, or better still, with I fisherman's knot (figure 16). Such a waistlength obviously reduces the chances of internal injury in the event of a fall. It is made of hemp because to use nylon could be dangerous – nylon has a low melting point and the friction of a nylon rope running over a nylon waistlength could lead to the latter melting. Waistlengths are sold ready made up with their ends whipped, for a few shillings each. Because hemp is a natural fibre it will rot and so whenever your waistlength gets wet it should be carefully dried before putting it away and it should be replaced from time to time.

The rope is attached to the waistlength by a krab and this should be a screwgate. It is extremely easy, when climbing, to lean forwards against an edge of rock, press open the krab gate and have your rope slip out, leaving you unprotected. For the same reason it is worth checking from time to time to see that the sleeve is screwed home.

Tarbuck invented a special knot to make full use of the stretching properties of nylon rope. It is tied in a generous loop. The secret is that the knot will remain stationary until it receives a shock load when it will slide, grudgingly, up to the karabiner. In other words, it acts as a kind of brake (figure 16).

The protection which a falling leader receives from this system is four fold:

1. The friction of the waist belay (as in the other system).
2. The jerk is reduced by the braking effect of the knot.
3. The extension of the nylon rope (as in the other system).
4. The easing of the body blow by wearing a waistlength.

All these help to soften the impact of a fall, though it must be borne in mind that the blow will still be a heavy one.

The Tarbuck System is undoubtedly the best yet devised for British rock-climbing. It does have disadvantages: first, the waist karabiner must be a good one (ASMU for preference) and secondly, the Tarbuck knot is difficult to tie, bulky, and can work loose especially on kernmantel rope. I am sorry to say that many climbers do not use the proper knot at all and so reduce their safety factor.

On the Continent, climbers usually tie on with a chest harness, but this method has never been popular in Britain because it is rather awkward on steep rocks. Recently, however, a number of special harness type belts have appeared on the market and these may become popular, especially in artificial climbing (figure 12c).

Karabiners also help to make the static belay easier to arrange. They allow separate loops of rope, known as slings, to be hitched around the anchor. This loop is then clipped onto the waistlength with a karabiner.

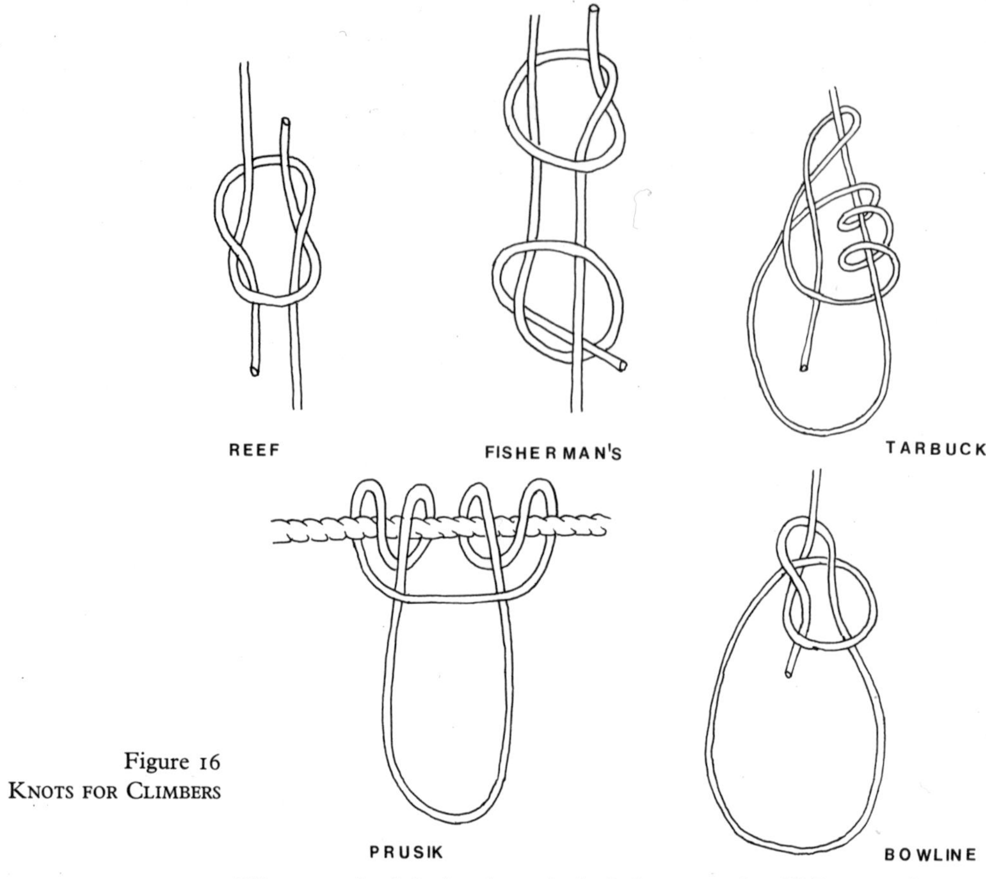

Figure 16
Knots for Climbers

The standard belay length is 8 ft or 10 ft of No. 4 nylon rope, specially made up for the job with its ends whipped. It is tied into a loop using a fisherman's knot. Alternatively a specially spliced abseil loop of No. 4 can be used, and is often preferred since the loop is needed for abseils anyway. The cost is about 15s.

A sling such as this will fit the vast majority of belays, especially on the easier climbs. It is the only sling which maintains the overall strength of your belaying system and so it should be used whenever possible. There are times, however, when such a large sling simply will not fit – it may be too thick to go round a chockstone, for example. In a case like this the alternative is to make two or even three static belays using 1″ wide nylon tape slings (breaking strain 3,000 lbs). If this won't work either, then you must seriously consider whether your stance is really suitable or

64

whether there is a better one just ahead. It is fatal to use thin or inferior slings for belays.

The belay karabiner should be a screwgate because, like your waist krab, it can so easily be pushed open accidentally. Figure 13*b* shows a sling belay – notice that the sling is attached directly to the waistlength and never to another karabiner, because a twisting motion of one krab against another could cause a pin to break on the gates.

Once you have a sling and karabiners at your disposal, all sorts of belays can be arranged, and some of these are shown in the illustrations. The point to bear in mind always is the likely direction of strain in the event of a fall.

The protection I have so far mentioned is engineered by the second for the protection of his leader (or vice versa) but the most exciting part of modern technique is the protection which a leader arranges for *himself*. It has helped to raise the standard of climbing in the last few years.

Supposing a leader fell when he was thirty feet above his second. Allowing that he does not land on a ledge at some point in between, then he is going to end up thirty feet *below* his second, at least – that is, a total minimum fall of sixty feet. Such a fall would be very serious indeed, so imagine what the consequences might be if a leader fell on a hundred foot pitch! The art of protection lies in reducing the distance a leader can fall.

This is achieved by the use of running belays, better known as runners. A runner consists of a sling placed over some spike, or round some tree or chockstone, with a krab at the other end through which the leader's rope passes (figure 17*a*). It is obvious how such a runner reduces the distance a leader can fall, and, as you may well imagine good runners inspire confidence.

A competent leader will use runners even on an easy climb if his run out is a long one. There is always the chance that he may be hit by a falling stone, or that a hold will come away, and it is better to be safe than sorry. Runners are also used to protect a particularly tricky move – in which case the runner is positioned as high as possible near the move.

Though runners are generally to protect the leader, he can also use them to protect his second in certain cases. For example, supposing a climb changes direction; without a runner the rope would go diagonally from leader to second and if the latter came off he would have a hair-raising swing across the rocks. If, however, a runner was placed at the very point where the change of direction took place then the second would be protected by a vertical rope for as long as possible. Such a situation exists on the first pitch of The Wrinkle, a popular climb in Llanberis Pass.

Another case is the long traverse, where the line of the climb is across the rocks. In such a case the second is virtually in the same position as the leader as regards safety and if the leader places runners they will both be protected. For a party of three, of course, the runners would be left on to protect the last man. Traverses like this can be found on Spiral Stairs and Crackstone Rib, both in Llanberis Pass, and the well-known Holly Tree Traverse on Raven Crag, Langdale.

Placing a good runner may not always be easy, and some that are easy may be useless because they are dragged off by the rope. The safest runners, of course, are those which

66

cannot be dislodged – trees and chocks, for instance. Spikes have to be examined critically: will the runner stay in place? There are no hard and fast rules for this: sometimes a tiny spike is quite secure and at others the rope slips off large bollards.

Once again, the No. 4 sling should be used whenever possible (or 11 mm perlon) with a krab turned so that the gate faces outwards away from the rock. It is easier to use ordinary krabs rather than a screwgate, but it still needs to be of maximum strength.

Once a leader puts on a runner the whole direction of the strain in the event of a fall is altered. Because the karabiner is now acting like a pulley the jerk will be *upwards*, and the second should be quite sure that his own static belay is capable of withstanding an upwards pull.

A glance at figure 18 will show you that a running belay has to stand up to twice the normal shock load in the event

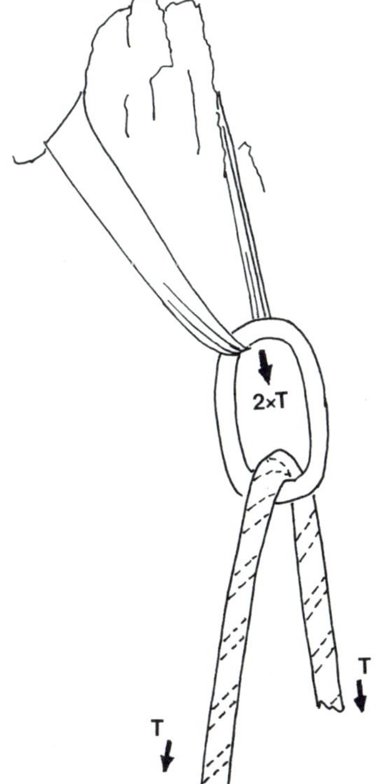

Figure 18
SHOCK LOAD ON A RUNNER. From the diagram you can see that if the tension in the rope is T lbs then the force transmitted to the runner by the krab is twice as much, and so runners and karabiners must be strong.

of a fall. If the fall is a long one there is a chance that the tremendous load will break the krab or the sling or even the rope. Because of this, a leader on a long run out should always take the precaution of placing a runner near the end of his pitch, if he has already placed one lower down, whether the difficulty warrants it or not.

Very often, the sort of spikes available for runners simply will not take a thick rope and climbers used to carry slings of thinner rope to cope with this. These slings were not very strong, but at least they were better than nothing. Recently, however, such slings have been replaced by nylon tape which will fit onto the smallest spike and stay put. The tape is as strong, or stronger, than the thin slings and because they will fit almost anywhere, it is often possible to place two tapes on a spike, thus doubling the security.

The use of tape is so recent that no standards have yet been agreed upon, but the following list gives the strength of tape commonly used. They are all two ply nylon webbing, and there are two varieties called soft and rigid.

$1''$ tubular tape	Soft	4,200 lbs
$1''$ flat tape	Soft	4,000 lbs
$1''$ flat tape	Rigid	3,000 lbs
$\frac{1}{2}''$ flat tape	Either	1,500 lbs

Though the tubular tape is stronger than its companion, there is a risk that it might roll off a spike under certain pulls, and my own opinion is that your most useful tapes will be $1''$ soft flat type, with some $\frac{1}{2}''$ for awkward threads. In the case of the latter, two runners should be put on for maximum security whenever possible.

Tape costs less than rope of a comparable strength. You will probably need at least half a dozen slings of various lengths from 4 ft to 8 ft. Two or three of these could be No. 4 rope and the rest tapes; the shorter ones. The rope is tied with a fisherman's knot, as I have already explained, but the tape requires a special knot like the one shown in figure 19.

Perhaps the most interesting development in recent years has been the use of cracks for holding runners. Trees and spikes are all very well, but they simply do not occur on

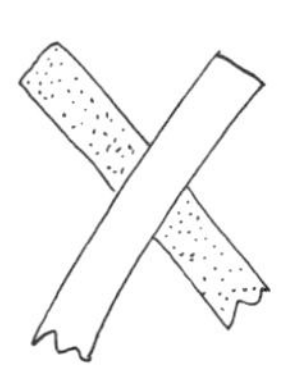
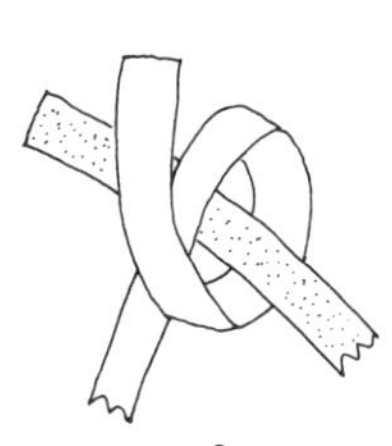
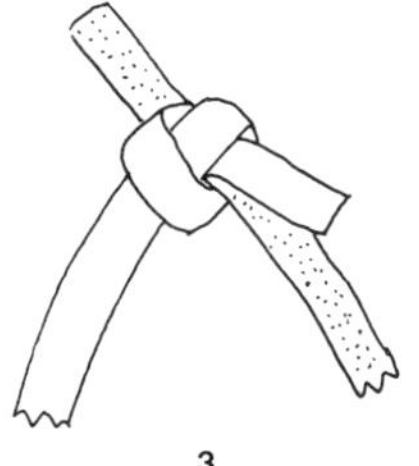
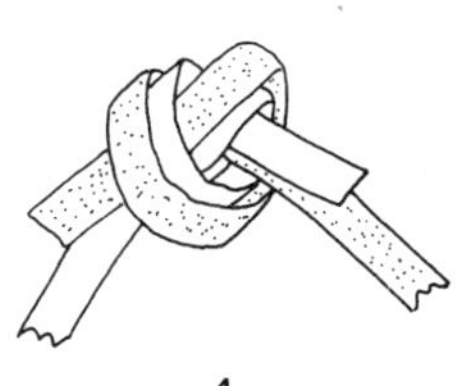

Figure 19
HOW TO TIE THE
NYLON TAPE KNOT

many climbs, whereas cracks are much more readily available. Basically, the idea is to push something into the crack which will lodge there, and thread a runner round it.

As an idea it was used as long ago as 1927, when stones were deliberately jammed into a crack on a hard climb in Wales, but the idea met with a certain amount of disapproval and was only revived recently.

At first the idea was to jam a steel nut into the crack; a nut with a thread bored out and a rope sling passing through it. Nuts jam very effectively – the harder you pull, the tighter they jam – but they can be awkward to take out again, and so various devices have taken their place.

I suppose one could call them all 'artificial chockstones' but they go under various disguises such as moacs, spuds, clogs, and crackers (figures 17*b* and 28). They cost between two and five shillings each, which is expensive for what they are, but they are certainly very effective.

There are two other ways in which cracks can be used for protection. One is simply to jam the sling into the crack by means of its knot, for which you need a favourably shaped crack and a lot of faith. The other extreme is to use a metal peg, or piton, hammered into the crack and to which a krab can be attached. There is a great reluctance to use pegs in Britain, particularly in the major areas such as the Lakes or Wales, and it is fairly certain that if a peg is needed on a climb that fact will be mentioned in the guide book. The method of placing pitons is dealt with in Chapter 7.

Most of our British crags have easy ways off – a climb up is generally followed by an easy walk down again, but there are places where this is not so: for example, the Inaccessible Pinnacle in Skye, Ilam Rock in Derbyshire or the celebrated

Napes Needle in the Lake District. On climbs such as these, getting up is only half the problem.

Climbing down always seems to worry beginners, though why this should be so is hard to fathom. The fact is that on the easier climbs, climbing down is easier than climbing up – for one thing you can see the holds better. Of course, there are exceptions to this, but it is very often true.

The same procedure is used in climbing down as in ascent. The descent is done pitch by pitch, with belays and runners, except that the leader comes down last, since this is the position of least security. It is the responsibility of his partner to see that adequate protection is placed for him.

Very easy rocks can be descended facing outwards or sideways – the less difficult parts of the Nevis ridges, for example, or the upper reaches of the Napes Ridges on Great Gable, but in general the usual position will be to face in and simply descend normally. Some experience is very worthwhile and is sadly neglected by many climbers. On crags such as the Napes or the East Face of Tryfan there is plenty of opportunity for climbing up one route and down another without undue difficulty.

When climbing down is too difficult, you can make an escape by sliding down a prepared rope by the method known as abseiling.

In the Alps, where abseiling is frequently necessary, a special rope of 9 mm kernmantel is carried for the purpose, but this is really not necessary for this country. Nevertheless, whenever an abseil is known to be part of the expedition, a spare nylon rope should be carried, otherwise you will have to use your ordinary rope and that will leave you unprotected.

The real secret of good abseiling is careful preparation. The rope is doubled and hung down the cliff from a belay block or a piton. The following points are most important:

1. Tie the loose ends of the rope together – this keeps them level and stops them splaying out on the rocks.
2. Make sure the coil will run free, hold the middle and cast the two ends out vigorously, well clear of the rock face. This should give it a free fall, without snagging. In a high wind it can be difficult to manage this but it helps to

weigh the ends with some pegs or old krabs.

3. Ensure the ends reach the ground or the stance you are aiming for.

4. Check your abseil point most thoroughly. It should not let the rope ride up but it should allow it to slide round easily – you will want to pull the rope down after you later. Of course, it must be absolutely sound: a good stout tree is probably the best abseil point you could have.

There are two well-known methods of sliding down the abseil rope. The most popular of these, because it is the most comfortable, is known as the sling and krab method (figure 20*b*). An abseil sling, which is a spliced loop of 7 ft length of No. 4 nylon, is twisted into a figure eight and you put one leg through each of the loops so formed. A screwgate krab is then clipped over the crossover and the whole thing drawn up to your thighs. The double abseil rope is then passed through the krab and over your left shoulder. You hold the rope which is in front of the krab with your left hand and the rope behind you with your right.

Allowing the rope to slide freely through the krab you walk backwards to the edge of the cliff and then slowly lean out against the tension of the rope, keeping your body rigid so that there is no bending of knees or hips. This takes considerable nerve the first time that you try it!

You must judge the moment of take off as being the time when you feel that it is possible to walk backwards down the rocks. You walk down calmly and deliberately, even turning slightly so that you are better able to judge which line to take.

The chief fault of most climbers, when abseiling, is to keep a tight grip on the rope with their left hand, i.e. the hand which is in front of them. It is a natural reaction, but unnecessary and painful because the rope burns your hand. In fact, you can let go with your left hand whenever you like without any effect, since it is your right hand which does the real work.

By varying your grip you can let the rope run as quickly or slowly as you wish, and if you bring your right arm in across your body you will even come to a halt – the friction

of the rope across your shoulder will see to that.

It is a good idea to see that the abseil sling is fairly tight, otherwise it pulls up to your chest and your clothes snag in the karabiner. If the sling is too long, as is often the case, it can be shortened by tying a knot in one end.

The second common method of abseiling is often called the classic method because it was the first one to be used. In this you rely entirely on the abseil rope without any slings or karabiners, and because of that it is a useful method to know. You stand astride the rope, facing into the rock, and lifting the rope from behind you bring it over your right hip, across your chest, over your left shoulder and hold it with your right hand behind your back (figure 20a). You then walk down the cliff as before. This method is just as

72

good as the other one but it does need rather more practice and you can get very sore if you do it wrongly!

Abseils can be made over the most spectacular overhangs. You will find that you are really sitting in a loop of the rope (or your sling, depending on the method you are using) and that contact with the rock is not really necessary at all. Using your controlling arm, you simply slide down the rope. However, abseils like this are rare in Britain and they need a certain degree of skill and nerve on the part of the climber. If you wish to practise 'free abseiling' as it is called, then my advice is to choose a big tree and try abseiling from the branches.

Good abseiling practice can be got at most of the outcrops. Choose a 30–40 ft slab for a start, and take the precaution of having a safety rope, that is, a normal climbing rope belayed from above. On long descents involving many abseils, experienced climbers wear their ordinary climbing rope the whole time, and use a special rope for abseiling as I have mentioned earlier.

The two methods which I have described are the easiest to learn and the commonest, but there are several other ways in which abseiling can be done. Some of these are best described as pure sensationalism. They should be left alone until you have a fair amount of experience. Similarly, there are special devices to make abseiling easier, called descendeurs, which are very useful in the Alps where abseiling is common, but not necessary in Britain.

Most young climbers enjoy abseiling, and it is undoubtedly good fun once you have mastered the technique, but it is terribly easy to become reckless and careless at it. Take care!

6 Leading

Your first climbs will be behind an experienced leader, but it need not be long before you are leading some of the easier routes yourself. It is important that you should, for this is the only way you can appreciate the leader's position and responsibilities.

As a leader you will find new delight and excitement. The feel of being on 'the sharp end' as it is often called, is quite different from that of being second man. The rope is below you, trailing down into dizzy depths, whilst you are all alone, inching your way upwards on tiny holds. Everything seems much steeper, and your mind concentrates sharply on the work in hand. It is only as a leader that you fully appreciate the meaning of exposure and lack of protection.

Your first responsibility as a leader in rock-climbing is to *yourself*. You are the key figure, and if anything happens to you then it is likely to affect the party as a whole. Because of this, you must climb within your powers and keep a sharp eye open for protection; time is of no consequence. If your second has to wait for an hour on a cramped ledge whilst you are tackling a difficult pitch, then that is just his misfortune – it is all in the luck of the game, and he should understand that.

At the same time you do have responsibilities to the rest of your party. First, it is your job to choose the correct line so that you do not go off route and lead everyone into unexpected difficulties. Then, too, it is your job to choose the suitable stances and belays from which to protect the party. Other jobs are placing runners for your second on a traverse, warning him about any sudden change of pace – if you are going to make a quick swing across a gap, for instance – and, if your second is a novice, you may even have the task of 'talking him up' a tricky pitch.

So you can see that a leader has quite a few things to think about. Because of this your first few leads are best done on climbs which you have already accomplished as a second, and which you know are well within your powers. If you can get an experienced climber to act as your second so much the better because it will give you more confidence and he will be able to offer advice if the need arises.

A leader must also be able to identify and follow the instructions given in the climbers' guide-books. These are specialised pocket-books cataloguing the climbs on a given crag or group of crags and they are sold in all the climbing equipment shops. They frequently make entertaining reading but their real purpose is to direct a climber to his chosen route and tell him the grade, length of pitches and any other information necessary for a successful ascent. What they do *not* do is tell you *how* to climb the route, except in very rare cases where some unusual move has to be made, such as on Rope Wall, Tryfan, where some peculiar lassoo tactics are required. Guide-books state the problem clearly, but the solution is left to you.

The commonest form for guide-books follows the pattern laid down by the great Lakeland climber H. M. Kelly who was editor of the guide-books produced by the Fell and Rock Club. This is sometimes called the 'pitch by pitch' description and here is an example, taken from a little guide-book which I produced some years ago for a crag called Pontesford, near Shrewsbury:

VARSITY BUTTRESS 210 *ft Severe.*

The classic route of Pontesford. A fine climb. Starts near the left end of the Fifty Foot Wall where this rises to a sharp crest. There are well marked holds, low down.

1. 60 ft. Climb the wall moving first to the right and then straight up on awkward holds. When the position eases move left to the sharp crest on the wall, which proves to be the end of an arête. Ascend the arête to a tree belay.
2. 40 ft. Easier but pleasant climbing follows the arête to the ledge beneath the Nose. Belay.

3. 30 ft. Walk left along the ledge into a small gully. Belay.
4. 80 ft. Taylor's Crack. Just right of the blank wall of the
   Nose there is a well marked crack which is ascended on
   good holds. Climb the ridge above to a definite finish.
   Belay (see figure 22.)

Most of the English and Welsh guide-books follow this formula, but those for Scotland are often less detailed. It is not uncommon to find a 600 ft climb on a Scottish crag described in two or three sentences, where an English guide-book would require at least a whole page. Some climbers prefer this more general approach but it would not work on our smaller English and Welsh crags because the climbs are much closer together than they are in Scotland.

The route descriptions are always supplemented by diagrams showing the line taken by the climb. These can be very useful, especially on the long gritstone edges near Sheffield (Stanage Edge is four miles long!) which are difficult to describe in words.

One or two points about guide-books are worth remembering. First, remember that climbs are graded for dry weather and rain might make them harder. Secondly, the length of pitch given in the book is the actual length of rope needed – for example, the vertical height of a pitch might be 20 ft, but in climbing it you may have to make a 10 ft detour, and so the length of the pitch becomes 30 ft. Right and left always mean as the climber faces the rock, but some books, in describing gullies, speak of *true* right and *true* left, which are geographical terms and mean in relation to the flow of the stream down the gully.

Perhaps the hardest decision which any leader has to make is that of retreat. It may be that you have bitten off more than you can chew, or perhaps it comes on to snow heavily, or somebody in the party is taken ill – sooner or later, something will arise which makes you think of retreat.

The first question to ask yourself is whether retreat is possible. On the easier grades of climbs the answer should always be 'yes' because you ought to be able to reverse any move you have made (your climbing down practice pays off here) but as climbs get harder they involve more committing moves which may make retreat extremely difficult. A move which is, say, Mild Very Severe taken from left to right, could well be Hard Very Severe when done in the opposite direction.

Theoretically at least, it ought to be possible to abseil off to easier ground and here again, on the harder climbs, some climbers carry a couple of pegs and a piton hammer for just such an emergency. This is an extreme solution, however, and you really need to be quite sure that retreat is the only thing possible.

Every pitch will not 'go' at a first attempt; like Bruce and the spider, you might have to try and try again. Don't be discouraged, for it happens to everybody. At the same time common-sense has a part to play and the climber who is always 'pushing it', or climbing beyond his limit, is likely to have a serious accident.

Retreat due to the illness of one of your party, or because of bad weather is rather different. Here the decision to be made is whether retreat would be *easier* than going on. Of course, bad weather need not affect your climb at all: retreat would only be contemplated if the weather was so bad that the standard of climbing was altered to beyond your capabilities – perhaps the holds become ice coated, for example – or on a long climb which you have just started and do not wish to continue in the rain.

As your climbing progresses you will start to modify your equipment to suit your own tastes. This is especially the case with boots. Today, many rock-climbers prefer to climb in very lightweight boots known as *kletterschuhe,* or klets.

Klets are a neat fitting boot with suede uppers and a very thin vibram sole, usually stiffened to give a more positive hold. They have stiffened toe-caps, too, and are made as narrow as comfort will allow.

On climbs where the holds are very small, or where there is a lot of toe jamming, klets have distinct advantages. Also, they are lighter and cheaper (about £4–5) than ordinary boots, and many climbers wear them in preference to proper mountain boots. They do have disadvantages, though. They are not waterproof, they are often uncomfortable to walk in (and prolonged walking in them spoils their stiffening) and they are not really cheaper in the long run because they do not last as long as proper boots.

Klets are very convenient for roadside crags like those in Llanberis Pass or Borrowdale, or many of the outcrops, but whenever much walking is involved it is better to carry them to the foot of the crag. This is scarcely worth the effort for anything less than Severe climbs.

Much more useful than the ordinary *kletterschuhe* is the canvas topped boot invented by the French guide Pierre Allain, and called simply, PA's.

PA's consist of a high canvas upper, very similar in appearance to a baseball boot, with lacing which goes right down to toe level. They have a smooth composition sole, narrow and with pointed toes (figure 21). They give a really excellent friction grip, can be used on the minutest holds and are admirable for jamming into cracks.

When they were first introduced it was considered necessary to have a very tight fit, and some climbers even wore them without stockings, but this idea is now discounted. Nevertheless, because of their narrowness they do become uncomfortable after a while and many climbers prefer to take them off in between climbs. They are not for

Figure 21
PA's. A favourite with rock-climbers. Notice the very narrow foot, pointed toe and high ankle. The boot can be laced tightly all the way down.

walking in, naturally, but because they are so light and the tops can be folded over, they are no bother to carry.

The smooth soles are not affected by wet rock, though they are at a disadvantage on rock which is greasy through mud or lichen, and their chief drawback comes not on the climb itself but on the descent afterwards – PA's are treacherous on wet grass or clay paths and great care is needed. The boots cost about £5 and there are now several similar types on the market.

Not so long ago it was considered as showing off if you wore PA's on anything but the hardest climbs, but the absolute convenience of the boots quickly made them popular with climbers of all standards, and now they can be seen even on very easy climbs. Many of the pictures in this book show climbers wearing PA's, but remember, they are not absolutely essential, whereas proper boots are.

Once you have done your first few leads on climbs with which you are familiar, you will be casting around for new worlds to conquer. For many young leaders it becomes a competition to reach the top grades as soon as possible. For some, who are gifted with great natural ability, it becomes a race to catch up with the current masters of the sport or even surpass them in skill and enterprise. Such climbers become completely absorbed in high standard climbing and often they will refuse to touch easier climbs, in case, by some chance, it lessens their confidence.

It is only by such fierce dedication that any sport can progress, and rock-climbing is no different from the rest in that respect. However, for every climber who reaches the top flight there are hundreds who remain content with less ambitious climbs. They are the climbers who simply like the feel of rough rock under a warm sun, the dizzy heights and the remarkable scenery. They gain their enjoyment from the great classic climbs which have stood the test of years, many of which are in the easier grades.

The principal areas for rock-climbing in England and Wales are the Lake District, the Peak District and Snowdonia. In Scotland, which is largely mountainous, the chief centres are Glencoe, Ben Nevis, the Cairngorms and Skye.

Some climbers are so fond of one particular area that they seldom go anywhere else; this is especially the case with Snowdonia, where there is a very high proportion of technically difficult climbs. In Scotland, the purely rock-climbing season is restricted to the summer months because winter snow lies long on the high bens. In fact, to obtain the fullest enjoyment from the Scottish crags you need to be an all round mountaineer.

Whatever area you choose to climb in, there will be detailed guide-books to the crags. These are frequently revised to bring them up to date, though often a new edition is quickly sold out and you may have to wait or buy a second-hand copy. Enquiries at your local climbing shop will tell you which are available. In addition there are three books which give an overall picture of the climbing in Britain:

1. *Where to Climb in the British Isles* by E. C. Pyatt
(Faber 20s.)
2. *Rock Climbing in Britain* by J. E. B. Wright (Kaye 16s.)
3. *The English Outcrops* by W. Unsworth (Gollancz 30s.)

The first of these is a gazeteer of all the crags in Britain, the second describes the crags in more detail and mentions some of the best climbs, whilst the last deals with the hundreds of local outcrops that dot our countryside.

These books are worth studying whenever you are planning a weekend's climbing or a long holiday. In the meantime let us look at the major areas in general from the point of view of a young leader who has reached V. Diff standard.

The Lake District

The mountains of the Lake District radiate out from the central hub – the Scafell group – like the spokes of a wheel, in-between which are the long and beautiful valleys for which the area is world famous.

The valleys provide the climbing centres and because of the way they are arranged it is seldom convenient to travel

Figure 22
Opposite page LEADING. The leader is tackling Taylor's Crack at Pontesford in Shropshire, a Severe. This is a fairly exposed move without protection.

80

from valley to valley; the usual practice is to climb on the crags of the valley where you are staying. Wasdale is the traditional home of English climbing and a fine centre but it is rather awkward to reach. More convenient are Langdale, Coniston and Borrowdale. There are also climbs in the valleys to the east, but the best of these are rather hard for a novice and the others scarcely make a visit worth while.

The best all-round centre for a young leader is Borrowdale, which has a wide variety of crags suitable for the V.Diff. man – Shepherd's, Bowderstone, Raven, Troutdale and others. It is also fairly easy to reach the high mountain crags of the Napes on Gable and the Buttermere climbs.

If you can lead to V.Diff. the Lake District has many good climbs, some of them not at all easy! Here are some well known ones which are well worth doing:

Woodhouse's Climb	Dow Crag	Diff.
Gordon and Craig's	Dow Crag	V.Diff.
Bowfell Buttress	Bowfell	Diff.
Rake End Chimney	Pavey Ark	Diff.
Cook's Tour	Pavey Ark	V.Diff.
Little Chamonix	Shepherd's Crag	V.Diff.
Donkey's Ears	Shepherd's Crag	V.Diff.
Bowderstone Pinnacle	Bowderstone Crag	V.Diff.
Troutdale Pinnacle	Black Crag	V.Diff.
Grey Knotts Face	Gillercombe	Diff.
Wall and Crack	Pike's Crag	V.Diff.
Slingsby's Chimney	Scafell Crag	Diff.
Moss Ghyll	Scafell Crag	V.Diff.
New West Climb	Pillar Rock	Diff.
North Climb	Pillar Rock	Diff.

Snowdonia

The rock-climbing in North Wales began in the Snowdon and Ogwen areas but has now spread to every corner of the region; even such unlikely places as Anglesey and the Lleyn Peninsula. Unlike the Lake District, there is no uniform pattern of valleys and on the whole Snowdonia is wilder and bleaker, with mountains which are just that little bit higher. Nevertheless, it is much more cut up by good roads than the Lakes and so there is not the same need to confine yourself to one particular valley.

Many of the climbs are very modern and very hard, on crags which hold no interest for the beginner – Gogarth, the huge sea cliff of Anglesey, being a case in point, and the same is true of the most famous crag in the area, Clogwyn du'r Arddu, known affectionately to climbers everywhere as 'Cloggy'.

For the beginner the best centre is still Ogwen because there is a marvellous range of climbs in the Diff. and V.Diff. grades within easy reach, including many of the famous classics. The popular crags are Milestone Buttress, East Face of Tryfan, and Idwal Slabs, but there are others almost as good such as Braich Ty Du.

There is a tremendous variety of climbs in Wales and the following list is only a sample:

Ampitheatre Buttress	Craig yr Ysfa	Diff.
Great Slab	Craig yr Ogof	Diff.
Gashed Crag	Tryfan	Diff.
Grooved Arête	Tryfan	V.Diff.
Milestone Direct	Milestone Buttress	Diff.
Hope	Idwal Slabs	Diff.
Tennis Shoe Climb	Idwal Slabs	V.Diff.
Route II	Lliwedd	Diff.
Avalanche	Lliwedd	V.Diff.
Flying Buttress	Dinas Cromlech	Diff.
Wrinkle	Carreg Wastad	V.Diff.

The Peak District

The High and Low Peaks embrace the southern limits of the Pennine Chain, and though mostly in Derbyshire, touch also the counties of Yorkshire, Cheshire and Staffordshire. Because it is so easily accessible to the heavily populated areas of the North and the Midlands, the Peak District, in terms of numbers, is the most popular climbing area of all.

There are two distinct parts. The High Peak is a region of wild windswept moors with dozens of weirdly eroded gritstone tors. These tors, and the crags known as 'edges', give superbly steep and difficult climbs of between 20 ft and 100 ft. Thus, they are often single pitch climbs. The rock – better known to non-climbers as millstone grit – is one of the best of all for climbing on, with superb friction.

Most of the larger outcrops have plenty to offer the novice and the best, from this point of view, are Stanage, Laddow, Cromford Black Rocks, Birchen's Edge and Castle Naze. The last two mentioned have very short climbs and are used extensively for training purposes.

The Low Peak includes the famous Derbyshire Dales and the climbing is on the spectacular limestone crags which fringe the dales and give routes of 250 ft or more. Unfortunately for the novice most of the climbs are fairly hard but there is some scope at Water cum Jolley, Chee Dale and Stoney Middleton. Deep Dale has plenty of less difficult routes, rather short, but admirable for getting to know about limestone.

There are more routes in the Peak District than in the rest of Britain put together, but as they are mostly short and even the difficult routes can be top-roped, there is no value in selecting a few from so many.

Scotland

Because so much of Scotland is mountainous the climbs are scattered over a wide area and many are difficult to reach. Climbers living in the Lowlands can make use of Arrochar and Glencoe for a weekend, and the Aberdeen climbers can get away to the Cairngorms, but for the most of us rock-climbing in Scotland means the long summer holiday.

Each area is so different from the others that it is impossible to describe Scotland as a whole. Amongst the popular areas are the jagged ridges of Skye, the most difficult mountains in the country, but with plenty of good rock-climbs suited to the novice, Ben Nevis with its long ridges, Glencoe with the splendid buttresses of Buachaille Etive Mor, the remote crags of the Cairngorms and the

weirdly shaped peaks of Arran. All of these have plenty to
offer the beginner.

It cannot be emphasised too strongly that climbing in
Scotland involves much more than the ability to scale rocks.
The mountains are the biggest in Britain, the rock-climbs
are the longest, and many of the crags are very remote.
Remember, too, that ice and snow may lie on the mountains
until well after Easter.

Here are a few of the Scottish rock-climbs which a novice
would enjoy:

The Great Ridge	Garbh Bheinn	Diff.
North Face	Buachaille Etive Mor	V.Diff.
Agag's Groove	Buachaille Etive Mor	V.Diff.
Western Buttress	Sgurr Sgumain	V.Diff.
Pinnacle Ridge	Sgurr nan Gillean	Diff.
Cioch West	Sron na Ciche	V.Diff.
Observatory Ridge	Ben Nevis	Diff.
Tower Ridge	Ben Nevis	Diff.

Other Areas

There are numerous outcrops throughout the length and
breadth of the country upon which climbs have been made.
Mostly the climbs are short, though a selection of longer
climbs, suitable for novices, can be found on the Cornish
cliffs, the Dewerstone in Devon, and Pontesford in Shropshire. Some of the long limestone climbs, such as those in
the Avon Gorge and at Malham, are only suitable for
experienced climbers.

Ireland also has its rock-climbs, though they are mostly
recent and a lot of them are hard. The chief centres are
Luggala and Glendalough in the Wicklow Mountains and
the Poisoned Glen in Donegal.

7 Artificial Climbing

There are occasions when the natural protection on a climb is simply not sufficient for the risks involved. It may be that there are no spikes for runners, that the cracks are not wide enough to take jammed slings or that there are no proper belay points. The climber's solution is to hammer in a metal peg, called a piton.

On the Continent, where climbs are very long and speed is necessary, pitons are used much more frequently than in Britain. In this country we regard them as a last resort: something to be used only when protection is essential and there is nothing else to hand. Usually this is only on climbs of a high grade – there are several climbs in the easy and middle grades where protection is lacking but where the climbing is not regarded as sufficiently difficult to warrant the use of pegs, as for example the final two pitches of Cook's Tour, a V.Diff. on Pavey Ark, Langdale.

But they are used, for instance, as a belay on the Main Wall Climb, Cyrn Las (Hard Severe) because no natural belay exists at that particular point and the situation is extremely exposed. Instead of tying on to a spike or chock you clip your belay loop on to the ringed head of the piton. Limestone climbs, in particular, make use of pitons for runners and belays because of the peculiar nature of the rock. Sometimes the pegs are used for direct aid – as hand or foot holds – as on the Unicorn, Carreg Wastad and North Buttress, Shepherd's Crag, two rather hard climbs.

Quite obviously, using pitons on ordinary climbs, or free climbs, as they are called, has its problems. If you can hammer in enough pegs then even the most difficult climb becomes very much easier, which is why we use pitons with great reluctance – after all, there is no merit in overcoming the difficulty by cheating. If pegs are required, then the guide-book will say so, and quite often they will be already in place.

Nevertheless, a knowledge of how to use pegs is very important, especially as you approach the harder grades. It may be that the original pegs left in some particular climb have become dangerously rusted, or even removed, and for this reason alone it is always worthwhile carrying a few pegs and a hammer on the hard climbs.

To try and describe the dozens of different pegs which are available for rock-climbing would be quite impossible. In general, however, there are two main types: knife pitons, which have a flat blade, and channel pitons which have blades with a U-shaped cross section. They are usually made of wrought iron and can be various lengths.

Pitons such as these have been in use for a number of years without much change in their basic design, but quite recently the Americans, who do a lot of peg climbing on the immense granite walls of the Yosemite in California, have introduced pegs made from a chrome molybdenum alloy (chromolly) which are superior to anything previously used.

Figure 23 shows a selection of American 'hardware' as they call it. The different shapes and sizes are meant to fit cracks of different widths and depths – the large bong, for instance, is for a very wide crack, whilst the tiny rurp is for a hairline crack. Because they are imported from the USA these pegs are rather expensive, but a number of British and Continental manufacturers are already bringing out their own chromolly pegs, though not yet in such a wide variety.

On a climb which might require just one or two pitons, they are carried attached to your waistlength by krabs, but if a lot of pegs are being carried then it is better to hang them in bunches from a sling worn bandolier fashion. Since a large number of krabs would be needed as well then crossed bandoliers, one with pegs and the other with krabs is a convenient arrangement. This distributes the weight evenly, yet leaves everything easily accessible (figure 27).

Pegs are driven into the rock by means of a special peg hammer which has a heavy head and a hickory or steel shaft.

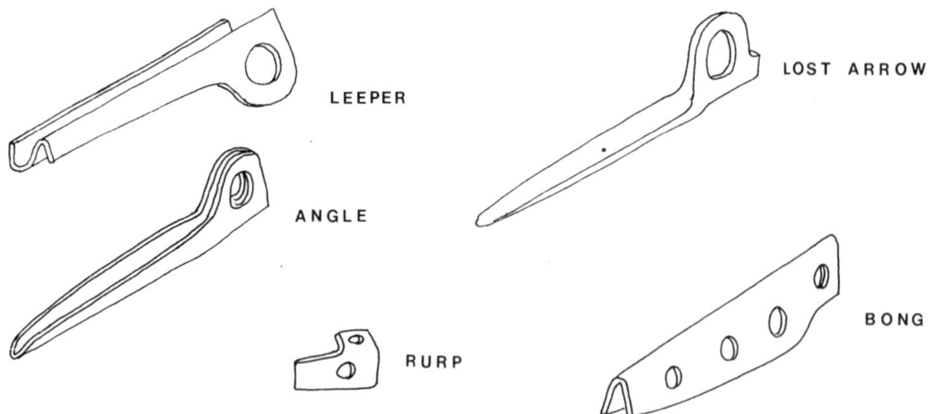

Figure 23

AMERICAN HARDWARE. A selection of chromolly pegs, cleverly
designed for various crack widths. The largest is the bong which gets
its name from the noise it makes when struck, and the smallest is the
rurp – Realised Ultimate Reality Piton.

The shape of the head does not matter much provided the
hammer is nicely balanced and gives a good swing. Ordinary
hammers are not very satisfactory – they break too easily.
A peg hammer costs about £1 (figure 28).

If you dropped your peg hammer during the course of a
climb, you could be in quite a fix. To ensure this does
not happen, the hammer is fastened to a long cord which
can be attached to a sling round your shoulder. Make sure
that the cord is long enough to enable you to reach at full
stretch with the hammer. When the hammer is not in use
it fits in the hammer pocket of your climbing breeches.

It takes a little experience to be able to judge the best peg
for a given crack. Trial and error is the only way until
such a time as a sort of sixth sense tells you instinctively
whether a crack is deep or blind. Limestone can be particularly infuriating in this respect, and so can some of the
new gritstone quarries where layers of rock flake away,
just as you think you have driven the peg home!

Other considerations being equal, a horizontal crack is
the safest for pegging. The rock will support the leverage
which may come onto the peg. For belay pegs especially,
a horizontal crack should be chosen whenever possible.

Unfortunately, vertical cracks are more numerous and so more frequently used. Here, only the friction between the peg and the rock holds it in place, but this can be quite satisfactory if the peg is properly driven home. Sometimes it is possible to choose a place where the crack narrows below the piton, and this gives it extra support.

Normally, pegs should be hammered home as far as possible. A sound peg gives a clear ringing note as it is driven home but a poorly placed peg sounds dull – it is not difficult to tell which is which. Before any real use is made of it, a karabiner should be clipped into the piton and given a couple of good pulls just to test it (figure 24a).

It sometimes happens, however, that a peg cannot be fully driven home – perhaps the only pegs you have are too long for the crack. Obviously, to use the eye of the piton under such circumstances puts a tremendous leverage on the peg and it may come out. To get over this difficulty you can use the so-called Hero Loops; short tapes fastened round the blade of the piton, where it joins the rock. This reduces the leverage (figure 24b).

Pegs can be driven into the most unlikely places by experts at the game – upside down in overhangs, in shallow pockets, or even in combinations to make what is virtually a thick peg out of two thin ones. These tricks of the trade can only come from experience, so much depends on the rock and the man who is doing the climbing.

Before American bongs came along, wide cracks were overcome by means of wooden wedges. Many of these can still be seen jammed in cracks, with their little nylon loops dangling like trade-marks. They should be treated with a good deal of care since they have often been in place for several years and are so rotten that they would collapse if any strain was put on them. Even if they are sound, you should try to avoid using the nylon loop – perhaps you could thread a tape behind the wedge, so making it into a chock, or you might be able to get a piton in alongside it. In any case, if you are forced by circumstances to use an old wedge, it is important to try and get additional protection as soon as possible.

One of the advantages of chromolly pitons is that they are

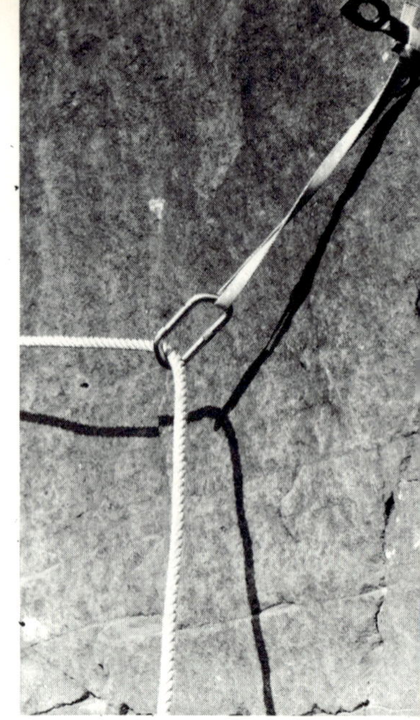

Figure 24*a* (*left*)
A WELL DRIVEN IN PEG. The peg is driven home as far as it will go.
Note the marking tape on the krab.
Figure 24*b* (*right*)
TYING OFF. A tape 'hero loop' being used as a runner. The peg cannot
be driven any further into the rock, so the tape loop is used to reduce
leverage.

easier to take out than the older type. The softness of the
metal in the latter meant that as the peg was hammered
home it would work its way round bends in the crack, and
though this often made the piton very secure, it could be
difficult taking it out. This is the prime reason why so many
pegs were left in place on artificial climbs.

You remove a peg by knocking it back and forth in
the line of the crack until it works so loose that you can
simply pull it out. As a general rule, all the pegs you put
in a climb should be removed by the last man as he comes
up. Permanent pegs – those which are supposed to be already
in place – should be left where they are.

In the principal mountain areas of Wales, the Lake District
and Scotland, there are very few climbs, or even pitches,
which rely entirely on pegs as a way up. On limestone
and some of the big gritstone quarries, on the other hand,
pegs are frequently used to overcome patches of rock

90

Figure 25
Twikker, Millstone Edge. This Derbyshire quarry has some very
good artificial climbs. Besides his two climbing ropes, the leader is
using a spare rope for gear hauling.

which would otherwise be unclimbable. It might be only a short pitch in what is otherwise a free climb, or it might be an ascent made entirely on pitons, such as Twikker on Millstone Edge, near Sheffield (figure 25). Climbs such as this are known as artificial climbs.

Artificial climbing (or peg climbing) came late to Britain. For many years it was regarded as a somewhat foolish pastime suitable only for Continentals and Americans until it was realised that we were denying ourselves some very good climbs simply because they included artificial pitches. Then too it was realised that artificial climbs give rise to some unique situations, unmatched even by the most exposed of free routes, as for example the great overhang of Kilnsey Crag in Yorkshire. As more climbers tried their hand at artificial climbing it quickly became apparent that it had difficulties and techniques all its own.

One of the difficulties is in grading the actual climbs. A scale beginning at A1 for the easiest and rising to A4 for the hardest is used in the guide-books, but this is really only a rough indication. The fact is that the difficulties can alter over the years; cracks become easier to peg, as in the case of London Wall at Millstone Edge, which began as A3 and is now much easier, or climbs become 'pegged up' which means that all the pegs are in place and an ascent is simply a matter of using them. Sometimes, of course, it works the other way – cracks becoming more difficult to peg.

The extra gear needed for an artificial climb, in addition to the pitons and hammer, is plenty of karabiners and two or three étriers.

Étriers are really little portable ladders made of rope with aluminium steps. Climbers usually buy the steps and make up their own étriers with thin kernmantel rope so that they can design them to their own fancy. Most have three steps, set eighteen inches apart, but some climbers prefer four.

The design for an étrier is shown in figure 26a. The steps are held in place by ordinary overhand knots underneath them, but they should be free to slide upwards because you will sometimes want to crouch on a lower rung and push the next one up out of the way of your knee. Below the bottom step the rope is tied off in a loop so that if necessary,

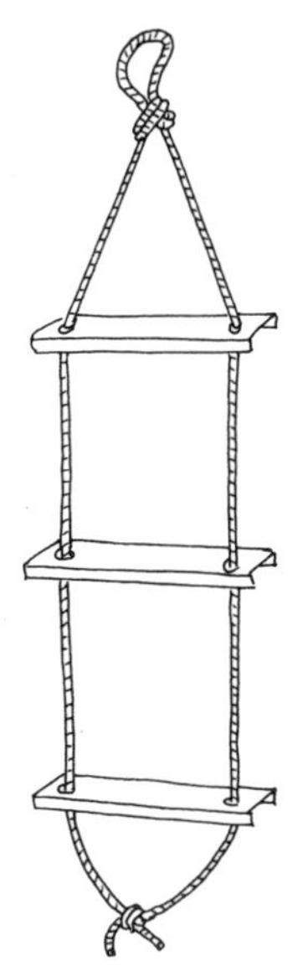

Figure 26*b* (*right*)
TAPE ÉTRIERS
Figure 26*a* (*left*)
ÉTRIER

one étrier can be clipped on to another.

Quite recently the traditional étrier has found a rival in the one made entirely of tape (figure 26*b*). These are certainly easier to carry and more comfortable to sit in when that is necessary, as it sometimes is, and they do not tangle quite as much as the metal steps. On the other hand, some climbers find them more difficult to use, claiming it is a struggle to get your feet into the loops.

A lot of krabs are needed in artificial climbing. These can be the same type as you would use on free climbs but on a long artificial route the weight is enormous, and don't forget you will be carrying pegs as well. Some of the load can be reduced by using alloy karabiners such as the PA which has a breaking strain of 5,500 lbs – strangely enough, stronger than most krabs, apart from the ASMU (figure 15*b*).

Let us imagine that once again you are at the foot of the rocks, this time about to lead your first peg climb. Very sensibly you have chosen a short and easy A1 – the Embankment at Millstone Edge, perhaps.

The first essential is to make thorough preparation, to have all the gear you need exactly where you need it. With this in mind you have three étriers clipped onto your waistlength,

Figure 27

two on one side and one on the other. Your peg hammer
rests in its pocket, secured round your shoulders by its cord
and you have crossed slings carrying pegs and krabs.
Around your neck you carry a couple of ordinary slings and
some tapes – the latter in case you need Hero Loops.

To your waistlength you fasten two ropes, one white and
the other red, equal in length, and to the front of your
waistlength you attach a little loop of tape – the so called
'cow tail'. You feel absolutely cluttered up! (figure 27).

You advance to the foot of the rocks, select a peg, and
reaching as high as possible, hammer it into the crack. Next,
you clip a krab into the peg and pass your white rope through
it. You then clip an étrier onto the peg and pull yourself up
onto the bottom rung. At this stage the red rope is simply
running free.

The next problem is to plant the second peg. This is where

94

the cow's tail comes in useful. You clip it onto the first peg, lean out on it so that you can balance, and you are now at liberty to use both hands.

When the second peg is in place you once again clip onto it a krab, but this time pass the red rope through it, calling at the same time 'Take in red!' You are now held in tension by the red rope from the peg above. You unclip your cow's tail, and calling 'Slack on white', move up onto the second étrier. You retrieve the étrier from below and continue as before.

Notice the sequence of moves – until it becomes automatic, you will find artificial climbing very slow work.

1. Peg.
2. Clip in rope.
3. Clip in étrier.
4. Move up.
5. Retrieve first étrier.
6. Cow's tail.

Two ropes are used because the drag of a single rope through numerous karabiners can be excessive, and they are coloured differently so that your second will be in no doubt as to which rope you want him to handle. It is possible to do a short artificial climb with just one rope, but generally speaking, two are better. Ropes can be purchased ready dyed, but it is a fairly simple matter to dye a normal white rope with a nylon dye.

The clipping of the rope through the karabiner needs careful watching. Clip the krab onto the piton then tip it over so that the gate comes round to the front. The rope must then be passed through it so that it runs from your waistlength in towards the rock and then down to the second. Failure to do this may result in rope jams or excessive drag.

Another cause of drag is when a peg is placed beneath the lip of an overhang. This can be overcome by using tape or even two or three krabs linked together to keep the rope away from the rock.

Clipping in and out of pegs can be a time consuming

business and sometimes, too, it is very awkward to retrieve the one below. To speed things up climbers have developed a sort of automatic system which relies on little hooks called fifis. These are permanently attached to the top of the étriers, and instead of clipping into a peg you simply hook on. But this is only half the story – as you step up your first étrier is pulled up behind you by a cord which attaches the fifi to your waistlength. On long artificial climbs fifis can save much valuable time, but my own opinion is that they are best left until after the basic techniques have been mastered. The cords can be quite a nuisance.

There are many stretches of rock where there are no cracks at all and it becomes impossible to use pitons. To overcome such blank rock it is necessary to drill holes and fit expansion bolts, to which is fitted a little metal bracket called a golo, which has a hole for taking a krab. Several big artificial climbs in this country rely on golos, among them the huge Central Wall of Malham Cove and great overleaning prow of Raven's Tor in Miller's Dale. However, this sort of work is usually only necessary on a first ascent and the vast majority of climbers have never placed a bolt in their lives (figure 28).

When it is done properly, artificial climbing is very safe, though it looks spectacular and leads the climber into some remarkable positions. After all, you are attached to the rock by numerous pegs, and provided your second knows his job there is little danger. Occasionally a peg might come out, and now and again one hears of 'unzipping' where several pegs come out one after the other, but this is fairly rare. Indeed, expert peg climbers often risk unzipping in order to achieve a speedy ascent – they deliberately plant the pegs only part way in and use Hero Loops to reduce the leverage, with one really well planted peg every so far for security. Not only does it make it quicker for the leader but it makes the second's job, of taking out the pegs, easier as well. However, it is not a practice to be recommended until you have considerable faith in your own abilities.

On a peg climb, the second gets little of the fun and most of the hard work. The leader belays in the normal way, though on a big climb his 'stance' may be his étriers and

his belay the peg. As he brings up the second, that poor chap has the job of taking out all the pegs, and collecting them together with the krabs ready for the next pitch. It can be a very tiring business.

It sometimes happens that artificial climbs are so over-hanging that if a leader falls he will be unable to regain the rock face, and will simply dangle on the rope. This can be very serious: within a very short time the constriction of the rope will cause him to black-out and he may even die. If there is any possibility of this sort of fall then the precaution of carrying prusik loops should be taken. Originally intended for crevasse resuce work in the Alps, prusik loops are a clever idea which allow a climber to climb up his own rope.

A prusik loop consists of No. 1 nylon rope, about 9 ft long, and tied with a fisherman's knot. It is attached to the main rope by a prusik knot (figure 16b) which has the admirable quality of being able to be pushed along a rope, but locking tight whenever a strain is put on it.

The first consideration, when hanging free, is to take the strain off your chest or waist. You attach a loop to the rope and stand in it – easier said than done. You then attach two more loops, one for the other foot and one which passes beneath your armpits and allows you to use both hands,

Figure 28
PROTECTION. Can you identify peg hammer, alloy krab, pegs, chocks, bolts and star drill?

97

which would otherwise be needed for hanging onto the rope. You can then slide the loops up in turn and so reach your last peg and the safety of the rock. Various devices have been invented to make prusiking easier, but unless you do a lot of difficult artificial climbing they are not really worth while for British climbing.

Even for climbers who may not wish to undertake out-and-out artificial climbs pegs make possible many moves which would not be practicable without them. Best known of these are the pendule and the tension traverse – both are ways of changing from one line of attack to another, such as from one crack to a parallel crack which is just out of reach.

In the pendule you plant a peg as high as possible, clip your rope into it with a krab, then swing across to the other crack, whilst your second gives you tension. The tension traverse is similar but not quite so spectacular: you push sideways against the pull of the rope and reach your objective in a sort of crab-like fashion.

By the time you are ready to begin artificial climbs you will undoubtedly have collected a considerable amount of equipment – pegs, hammer, krabs, slings, tapes and so on, and the trouble is that it will look exactly like everybody else's gear. Equipment inevitably becomes mixed, and especially on artificial climbs, so climbers mark their gear so that it can be distinguished from the rest without much trouble. Brightly coloured plastic tape of the sort sold in electrical shops is very good for the job, but make sure your friends use a different colour!

8 Mountain Safety

A good deal of rock-climbing takes place on crags which are in wild country, with little habitation, and sometimes a long way from the nearest road. Under conditions like these sudden illness or accident can be very serious and a climber must know what to do about it.

Natural illness such as a blinding headache or stomach upset is a wretched piece of bad luck, which can strike anybody. It can curtail a day's enjoyment, but this must be accepted: the trouble lies in trying to carry on as though you were perfectly well when the obvious remedy is to rest and take an aspirin tablet.

It is very difficult to make hard and fast rules about minor illnesses because people vary so much – there are even those who *always* feel rotten in the mornings, then buck up wonderfully as the day goes on. Generally speaking though, it is not wise to set off for a strenuous day on the crags if you do not feel up to it. This may not be as bad as it sounds – with luck it can mean no more than a change of crag. For example, it might be foolish to set off for Craig yr Ysfa at 9 a.m. if you have a bad headache, but by 11 a.m. you may have recovered, and there would still be time for climbing on a less remote crag, such as Tryfan.

A small first-aid kit should be carried by any party of climbers. It need not be bulky or heavy, just having the things which are necessary for minor injuries. It would include a selection of adhesive plasters for blisters and scratches, aspirin, lint and bandages for larger cuts, antiseptic cream, a few safety-pins and a small pair of scissors. In Scotland, during the summer months, it is also necessary to carry insect repellant – the midges and clegs (horse flies) are ferocious.

Apart from illness and minor mishaps, what else is there

that might go wrong on the hills? There are three unfortunate possibilities:

1. You might lose your way and have to spend the night out – a forced bivouac.
2. Due to bad weather, poor food, long exertion, you may suffer from exposure. (This may be combined with 1 and 3.)
3. You may have an accident such as a fall, hit by a stone, or a twisted ankle.

Proper equipment and good training can prevent most of these from ever happening, but at the same time, you must know what to do in the event of an emergency.

Most of the crags in England and Wales are so frequently visited these days that well worn paths lead directly to them from the valley, and in good weather it is scarcely possible to get yourself lost. Even in poor conditions, crags such as Shepherd's or Dinas Cromlech are not difficult to find or escape from, since they are near the road, but those which entail a long walk, such as Scafell, Craig yr Ysfa, Kinder Downfall or practically any of the Scottish crags can be very tricky. Snow can obscure paths and mist throws everything out of perspective. I once knew of some climbers who set off in heavy rain to climb on Buachaille Etive Mor and failed completely even to find the mountain!

Some people have a very good sense of direction, but put them in a thick mist or a snow storm and their sense of direction vanishes. This is because the hundreds of little clues which their senses automatically pick up in clear weather – direction of the sun, the wind, lie of the land and so on – no longer are available. Only the accurate use of map and compass can show the right way.

An Ordnance Survey map of the 1 inch or $2\frac{1}{2}$ inch series and a compass of the Silva type should be carried whenever you are visiting a crag which is more than a few hundred yards from a road. Learn how to use them, and in this respect I can strongly recommend the new sport of orienteering as being good fun combined with first rate map practice.

Providing you have the correct gear, a night out on a crag or mountain, under normal summer conditions, need not be

Figure 29
AIDS TO NAVIGATION.
Map, pedometer,
and compasses. The
Silva type
transparent compass
is standard for
mountain
navigation and
orienteering.

a harrowing experience. Indeed, if you choose a fine night it can be very pleasant, but a forced bivouac, brought about because darkness has caught you out, indicates bad planning, poor map reading, or some injury.

Obviously the chief thing is to keep warm, and this means finding a bivvy place which is sheltered from the wind. If this is not possible, a long polythene bag, worn like a sleeping sack, will keep you warm, though it can give a lot of condensation. Another alternative is to have a rucksack which is fitted with a bivvy sheet.

The time drags slowly on a forced bivouac, especially the first few hours when sleep is difficult to find. If you are carrying a stove and have access to water, then 'brewing-up' is a popular way of passing the time.

If you are forced to bivvy on an actual crag face, you should keep the rope on and make sure that you are belayed throughout the night, even to hammered in pegs if necessary. Climbing on remote crags, particularly in winter, demands all-round mountain competence. You must be prepared for bad weather, expecting the worst though hoping for the best.

My own experience of the remote hills of Skye, for example, has been singularly fortunate – cloudless weeks of fine weather – but that does not mean that each time I go there I neglect to carry my bad weather kit, for I know that conditions in Skye *can* be terrible.

The point to bear in mind always is that if you are caught in bad weather on the remote crags you may be in for a fight against the elements lasting several hours. It is one thing to retreat from, say, the Black Rocks of Cromford, where you can be down on the road inside five minutes, and quite another to retreat from Ben Nevis.

You must equip yourself for survival. In addition to the gear mentioned in the first chapter the following are necessary:

Summer: 6 × 3 ft polythene bag, emergency rations, spare sweater, torch.

Winter: the above, plus, gloves and overmitts, balaclava, ice axe (if there are snow conditions) and a duvet jacket. This last is an eiderdown filled jacket which is superbly warm, and though not absolutely essential (they are very expensive), is the ultimate answer to cold weather. A duvet is especially useful on a bivouac (figure 30).

Food is always important on a long day's outing, particularly since most of the time is spent in strenuous activity. A supply of energy must be maintained; preferably energy which is easily assimilated by your body. For this reason the standard sort of pack lunch, consisting of meat or cheese sandwiches, is not really satisfactory since it is often indigestible – if there must be sandwiches it is better that they should be of jam or honey. Better still is to carry a supply of food which can be nibbled throughout the day: biscuits, fruit of all kinds, nuts and chocolate. A small, but regular energy input is better than a single stodgy snack.

In addition a reserve should be carried and kept for emergencies. Barley sugar or Kendal mint cake are very good for this, though it sometimes needs will-power to keep it in reserve! A friend of mine once kept an air-tight packet of emergency rations in his rucksack for eighteen months.

Many was the time he was tempted to eat it, especially since he always returned from his climbs in good time. Then, quite unexpectedly, he was forced to spend the night out on the mountain – and you can imagine how thankful he was that he still had his emergency rations to sustain him!

If your chosen climbing place is very remote indeed, as it could well be in Scotland, you would be well advised to have a minimum of four members in your party and to organise the emergency rations on a party basis. Here are the emergency rations which one of the Outward Bound Schools issues. They are meant to sustain four boys in bad weather:

6 oz sugar, 1 bar mint cake, 1 packet of chocolate, 1 tube of cheese spread, 1 tube of condensed milk, 4 small packets of coffee, 6 Oxo cubes, 8 oz wholemeal biscuits, matches, Primus and pan.

Long treks, bad weather, and poor food can easily lead
to exposure, which is a very serious condition. It is caused
by a lowering of the body temperature (98.4°F) and in
severe cases can result in death.

The extremities of our bodies – arms, legs, ears, nose,
and our skin – are never at as high a temperature as the core
of the body itself. Since heat flows from warm to cold
regions, this means that our body heat tends to flow towards
these extremities. Under normal conditions this does not
matter because the body receives more heat from the food
it consumes and from insulation of the clothes, but when
this new heat is not forthcoming, then the core of the body
must become colder and trouble sets in. Obviously, then,
the main body must be kept warm and anything which
tends to make heat flow towards the skin or limbs must be
avoided. This includes rubbing, warming, and alcohol.

The immediate treatment for exposure is to get the entire
body as warm as possible and to cut out heat loss. The victim
should be protected from the wind, of course, and wrapped
in plenty of warm clothing – duvets and sleeping bags if
possible. He should be protected from the cold ground by
insulating material (heather is good) and a fit companion
should lie with him to keep him warm. In severe cases it
may be necessary to give mouth to mouth resuscitation.

There can be no question of carrying on and hoping for
the best – men have died from exposure within a stone's
throw of habitation because of this. Take the proper pre-
cautions, then fetch help.

Tragically, exposure is not easy to determine in its early
stages, but the following symptoms should be watched for
whenever you have a particularly long and tiring day:

1. Unusual behaviour, unreasonableness, violent swearing.
2. Excessive feeling of tiredness, falling down.
3. Lack of concentration, failure to understand what is
   being said.
4. Slurred speech.
5. Shivering fits, constant complaints of coldness.
6. Sudden outbursts of energy.
7. Defective vision (this is very serious).

It cannot be emphasised too strongly that prevention is better than cure. On a long trek then:

1. Take plenty of spare clothing.
2. Take plenty of spare food.
3. Do not carry excessive loads – never more than 40 lbs.
4. Do not 'push it' under bad conditions.

Anything which curtails vision on a mountain is dangerous because it could contribute to exposure or benightment, or both. The most common form is mist and hill fog. but a snowstorm can have the same effect and a white-out, when the earth and sky merge into one indistinguishable white space, really has to be experienced to be believed.

Getting off the top of a crag in such conditions can be a trying experience, even if the ground is familiar. There is no easy answer to the problem. If the mist is a passing thing, which has come and gone several times during the day, then it may be feasible to find a sheltered nook and try and sit it out, but the risk of benightment and the general weather conditions would need to be considered. Alternately, you might abseil down the climb you have just completed, but this too is not always practicable.

The most reasonable compromise is for the party to remain roped together, separated one from another by about fifteen feet. Carrying the spare rope coiled in their hands they advance carefully in the least dangerous direction as indicated by the map and compass. On Scafell, for example, this would be towards the grassy slopes overlooking Burnmoor – a considerable detour, but much safer than trying to find Lord's Rake or Broad Stand, the usual quick ways down.

This method is certainly not infallible, and great care must be exercised at all times. It is tiring and frustrating and can call on great reserves of stamina and nervous energy.

Before setting out on any climbing expedition you should try and let somebody know where you are going and what time you expect to return.

In all the mountainous areas of this country there are volunteer Mountain Rescue Teams, who make it their job to organise the rescue of anyone missing or injured in the hills. Each team has Mountain Rescue Posts, which act as a sort of headquarters and store the specialist equipment. The Rescue Post may be a Youth Hostel or a hotel – its position is clearly shown on Ordnance Survey Maps and details are given in the local guide-books. In addition, it carries a distinctive badge in a prominent position, bearing the words RESCUE POST in large letters. Some of the more remote crags, such as Dow Crag and Scafell, also have Rescue Boxes for immediate use in the event of a mishap.

A Rescue Team is under the charge of a local mountaineer who knows the area thoroughly. It is his responsibility to organise the search or rescue, and if need be seek special help from outside bodies such as the Police or the RAF Mountain Rescue Service. The regular team members are usually local farmers or quarrymen (and keen local climbers as well) who sometimes have to give up a day's pay, or lose a night's sleep, in the line of duty. It is usual for any climbers in the vicinity of a rescue to give whatever help they can to the team.

If an accident occurs to someone in your party, you will have to take calm but urgent action on two counts: first, to ensure the immediate future safety and comfort of the victim, and secondly, to fetch help.

A knowledge of first-aid is a valuable asset for any climber to have. In extreme cases it can even save life, but even in less drastic circumstances, first-aid can make the injured person more comfortable and ease pain. As a minimum requirement you should be able to distinguish between serious injury and the less serious – this is not always obvious, because some quite superficial injuries can make a gory mess which looks bad. Of prime importance is to recognise spinal injury or internal injury. In the first case the victim should not be moved until expert help has arrived and in the case of internal injury, no drinks should be given.

In every case the injured person must be made as warm and comfortable as circumstances will allow. If he can be moved without further injury, he should be put in a place sheltered from the wind, or on a ledge where it is possible to build a wind-break around him. A tent, or a bivvy tent (a lightweight shelter carried by mountaineers making long winter ascents) would make an ideal shelter. Unless internal injuries are suspected, a warm drink would be beneficial, but no alcohol. (Remember that exposure may enter the situation – it might be hours before the rescue team arrives.)

On most of the popular crags, particularly in summer, help is seldom far away. It is one of the unwritten rules of the mountains that *everyone* answers a distress signal, and crags in these days are seldom deserted.

The Mountain Distress Signal is best given by whistle during daylight or whistle and lamp at night. The signal is:

Six blasts (or flashes) at ten second intervals, followed by a minute's pause, then repeated.

If your signal is observed the correct reply is:

Three blasts (or flashes) at twenty second intervals followed by a minute's pause.

If you have no whistle then anything which will attract attention can be used, such as shouting or waving an anorak. There are even special flares available, known as Miniflares.

However, if your signal is not answered you will have to make a descent to the valley, *even though it may mean leaving your injured companion alone.* Uninjured novices with the party may well be rather frightened by the turn of events, and the first task is to see that they are brought to a safe place. One, or two, people must make a swift but careful descent to the valley – this is no time for rashness; the injured person is depending on you.

Having reached the valley make immediate contact with the Rescue Post (by phone if that is quicker) or failing them, the police. They will want to know:

1. The exact position of the victim. If he is on a crag they will want to know which climb and even which pitch. (From this they can work out whether to effect the rescue from the top of the crag or the bottom.)
2. The time of the accident, and how many are involved.
3. Your estimate of the injuries.

They may ask you to go back with them, but if you are too exhausted this will not be possible. Some marker – a trailing rope, a bright anorak – should have been left to indicate the place of the accident and guide the rescue team.

As more people each year take up mountaineering, so the number of accidents increases. The sad fact is that most of them are caused by ignorance and incompetence – inadequate equipment and sheer carelessness.

A famous Italian climber once said, 'We go to the mountains to live, not to die'. What he meant was that if you learn the craft of climbing properly and take the necessary safeguards, you will enter on an exciting new life, the like of which is beyond imagination. But to try and reach for the heights without proper preparation is to invite tragedy.

Note: Useful booklets on safety are:
Safety on Mountains (CCPR, 26–9 Park Crescent, NW1. 1s. 6d.)
Mountain Rescue & Cave Rescue (Mountain Rescue Committee.
   1s. 6d.)
Junior First Aid (British Red Cross Society. 3s. 6d.)
Exposure (G. Outram & Co Ltd, Castle Douglas, Scotland. 8d.)

Some Useful Addresses and Publications

Association of Scottish Climbing Clubs (ASCC), 406 Sauchiehall Street, Glasgow, C2.

British Mountaineering Council (BMC), 74 South Audley Street, London, W1.

These are the representative bodies dealing with all aspects of British mountaineering. They will answer queries, but make sure first that the information cannot be obtained from the journals (see below) or a public library.

Climbing Courses

Training in rock-climbing, and general mountaineering, are offered by the organisations listed below. In addition to these there are many local education authority centres, Outward Bound Schools, and smaller private concerns which offer training. Lists of these, and advertisements, appear in the journals.

CCPR, 26–9 Park Crescent, London NW1.

CHA, Birch Heys, Cromwell Range, Manchester 4.

Holiday Fellowship, 142 Great North Way, Hendon, London NW4.

Mountaineering Association, 102a Westbourne Grove, London W2.

Ramblers' Association, 124 Finchley Road, London NW3.

Scottish CPR, 4 Queensferry Street, Edinburgh.

Scottish YHA, 7 Bruntsfield Crescent, Edinburgh 10.

YHA, Trevelyan House, St Albans, Herts.

Journals, etc.

There are a great number of journals and news sheets brought out by the various clubs, but usually only of interest to members. New climbs in the principal areas are given in the journal of the senior club for that area: *Climbers' Club Journal* (Wales), *Fell and Rock Club Journal* (Lake District), *Scottish Mountaineering*

Club Journal (Scotland), and *Irish Mountaineering* (Ireland). These are published annually and are obtainable from good climbing shops.

Articles of more general interest appear in:
Mountaineering. (Bi-annually 2s. 6d.) Published by the BMC, 74 South Audley Street, London W1.

This is the 'official' BMC magazine. Gives reports of tests on equipment, etc. Gives full list of clubs and training centres.
Mountaincraft. (Quarterly 2s. 6d.) Published by the MA, 102a Westbourne Grove, London W2.

The 'official' magazine of the Mountaineering Association, one of the oldest and largest training organisations.
The Climber. (Monthly 2s.) Published by G. Outram & Co Ltd, Castle Douglas, Scotland.

An independant magazine covering every aspect of the hills, from rock-climbing to ski-touring.
Rocksport. (Bi-monthly 2s.) Published at 41 Salisbury Road, Cardiff.

A very modern magazine devoted entirely to rock-climbing.

All these magazines can be purchased from any climbing shop or ordered through the post.

Some books worth reading

The standard text-book covering every aspect of mountaineering, and invaluable for reference is:
Mountaineering, A. Blackshaw, Penguin. 18s. 6d.
The following are autobiographies, biographies and background stories of famous climbs:
Commando Climber, M. Banks, Dent. 18s.
Mountaineering in Britain, Clark and Pyatt, Phoenix. 45s.
British Crags and Climbers, Pyatt and Noyce, Dobson.
Mountaineering in Scotland, W. H. Murray, Dent. 30s.
Undiscovered Scotland, W. H. Murray. Dent.
Because it is There, W. Unsworth, Gollancz. 21s.
Space Below My Feet, Gwen Moffat, Hodder & Stoughton. 18s.
High Peak, E. Byne, Secker & Warburg. 32s.
The Hard Years, J. Brown, Gollancz. 42s.
I Chose to Climb, C. Bonington, Gollancz. 30s.
Rock and Rope, S. Styles, Faber, 25s.
Rock-Climbers in Action in Snowdonia, Cleare and Smythe. Secker & Warburg. 35s.

Index